C000279732

Aspects of
ALFRISTON

Patricia Berry
and
Peter Longstaff-Tyrrell

S.B. Publications

First published in 2006 by S.B. Publications
Tel: 01323 893498.
Email: sbpublications@tiscali.co.uk

Email: peter.longstafftyrrell@tesco.net

ISBN 978-185770-325-2

Contents

Introduction

Records of the Alfriston neighbourhood go back in degrees to medieval times and illustrate an intriguing saga of transition for the community. Times have been harsh there, periodically the quality of life was very low in the backwater. From the early 1800s a fresh economy arrived, with the presence of troops, after which it then ebbed badly. A century later the village unknowingly re-invented itself as a tourist haunt nestling between the coast and Downs. Nowadays it is a mecca for visitors most of the week . . .

Aspects of Alfriston has strived to bring together a cross-section of topics for the reader who likes to browse through a book - as well as having ample authentic scenes. Similarly in 2006 the Charter 600 celebrations were the climax of months of planning to welcome residents and visitors to share everything that is so good about the varied Aspects of Alfriston.

Patricia Berry and Peter Longstaff-Tyrrell
have written over twenty books covering Sussex and Surrey local studies.

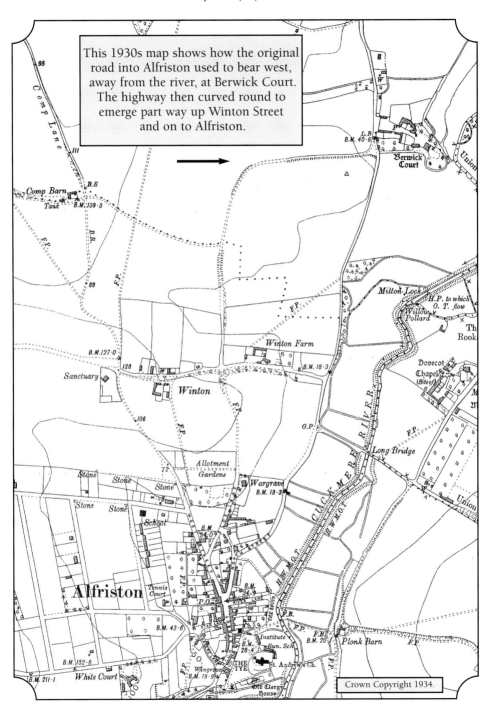

This 1930s map shows how the original road into Alfriston used to bear west, away from the river, at Berwick Court. The highway then curved round to emerge part way up Winton Street and on to Alfriston.

Crown Copyright 1934.

List of sources and further reading

ALFRISTON
Ronald M. Boyd. Goldleaf Partnership 1989.

ALFRISTON
A. Cecil Piper. Frederick Muller 1974.

ALFRISTON & THE CUCKMERE VALLEY.
Sandy Hernu. S.B. Publications 1992.

ALFRISTON MARKET DAYS
Juliet Clarke 2006.

ALFRISTON PAST AND PRESENT
W.H. Johnson. S.B. Publications 1998.

ALFRISTON TODAY AND YESTERDAY
Edna and Mac McCarthy. Drusillas 1982.

ALFRISTON AND DISTRICT
Patricia Berry
European Library, Zaltbommel/Netherlands 1992.

EAST SUSSEX LIBRARY SERVICE

EAST SUSSEX RECORD OFFICE

EASTBOURNE HERALD AND GAZETTE

"FIVE AND TWENTY PONIES"
Edna and Mac McCarthy. Drusillas

HISTORY OF ALFRISTON
Florence Pagden. Combridges, Hove 1950.

KELLY'S DIRECTORIES

PIKE'S BLUE BOOK DIRECTORIES

RECOLLECTIONS OF A SUSSEX PARSON
Rev Edward Boys Ellman. Country Books 2004.

REFLECTIONS FROM THE CUCKMERE VALLEY
Peter Longstaff-Tyrrell. Gote House Publishing 2004.

RON LEVETT. www.alfriston.line.co.uk

SUSSEX EXPRESS AND COUNTY HERALD

TALES FROM THE PARISH PUMP
David Arscott. S.B. Publications 1994

THE CUCKMERE - ANOTHER SUSSEX RIVER.
Edna and Mac McCarthy. Lindel Organisation 1981.

This pair of splendid signs on the Tye, representing the village past and present, was created by Litlington artist Penelope Ellis and wood-carver the Reverend Frank Fox-Wilson - involving around 200 hours work.

Derivations

ALFRISTON :
From Tun (farmstead) belonging to Aelfric (South Saxon name).
Orig. Alvricestone (Domesday 1086).
Traditionally pronounced Awlfriston and earlier Ahson town.

HIGH AND OVER :
From Hean Ofre (High Bank).
Orig. Heyovere (1287) then Heghenovere (1352) then Hindover
(Ordnance Survey 1824).

FROG FIRLE :
From Fierol (Saxon meaning Oak Covered).
Orig. Ferle (Domesday 1086) then Froggeferle (1288).

LITLINGTON :
From Tun (farmstead) belonging to Lytela.
Orig. Variously Litlinton, Litleton and Litelington (12th century).

LULLINGTON :
From Tun (farmstead) belonging to Lulla (South Saxon name).
Orig. Lullinton (1192). Archaic pronunciation Loynton.

WINTON :
From Tun (farmstead) belonging to Wiga (South Saxon Name).
Orig. Wigentone (Domesday 1086) then Wengeton (1223) then
Wynton (1548).

CUCKMERE (RIVER) :
From Mere (O.E. lake, pond or M.E. moor) and Cuca (pers. name) or
Cucu (O.E. for living). An original meaning for quick, something
alive. *cwicu mere* Cookemere (1335), Cokemer(e) (1352), also
Coukmere, Cuckmer (1586) then Cockmare (1724).

CUCKMERE HAVEN
Never an actual harbour, just a bay. Cokemerehaven (1352), haven of
Kockmare (1582).

1. *The Cuckmere*

Relaxing by the Willows Tea Gardens in the 1930s.

MOODY OLD RIVER

The tidal waterway is seen towards St Andrew's in flood and with turbulence at Burnt House Brooks . . .

At times the Cuckmere is becalmed and idle . . .

Summer 2005 - the tributaries at Gypsy Corner were choking with North American duckweed fern.
The following spring the water ran clear again.

EXPERIENCING THE CUCKMERE

The river was notorious for seasonal floods and during the 1930s contractors commenced remedial work from Milton Lock through to Litlington. Utilising three Ruston Bucyrus RB10 excavators, in drag line format, flood banks were created with mud dredged from the river bed, the western side banking being made a yard higher than the east.

New bridge works were undertaken at Plonk Bridge and with Long Bridge widened for access to Litlington. A raised footpath was created opposite The Willows car park and alongside White Way near Burnt House. The river is seen above in flood, off Plonk Bridge towards Frog Firle, in late 2005.

Commuter country - the bustling A27 crossing at Sherman's Bridge dates from the 1820s turnpike era. The river crossing was named after a local land-owning family named Sherlye. On 1875-1929 maps it is shown as New Bridge.

BRIDGES OF CUCKMERE

Long Bridge is said to have been a Saxon wooden footbridge, on poles over the river. The river was much wider then, hence the name. Now also known locally as Red Bridge it was extended both sides in the 1930s.

Plonk Bridge, aka White Bridge, is depicted during a previous generation when sailing barges still used the river. The large building to the left is the River Lane abattoir. The lane was also known as Slaughter House Lane and Butchers Lane.

CUCKMERE FOOTBRIDGES

Ancient Plonk Bridge was reconstructed in the 1930s and again during 2000. It is also referred to as White Bridge.

The modest bridge at Burnt House Brooks, Litlington, (below) crosses an often turbulent part of the river. This bridge is also known as White Bridge, but it has not seen any such paint for many years . . .

CROSSING AT FROG FIRLE

New Bridge at Frog Firle is known locally as Black Bridge and is used primarily by farm traffic, but it serves as a convenient venue for ramblers.

Poignant signs of bridging and sheep dips from centuries past are evident at certain locations along the banking. The tidal sweeps take their toll along the river side.

EXCEAT AND THE HAVEN

The thoroughfare at Exceat on the A259 remains open to single lane traffic as a means of traffic calming, keeping vehicles back on the A27.

The iron bridge was erected in the early 1860s to replace a stone bridge. In the late afternoon of August 31st 1940 the structure was fired upon twice by German submarine U91, as a token target during a recce of the Sussex coast.

Panoramic Cuckmere Haven where there ought to be a public footbridge - enabling travellers to enjoy fully the coastal paths.

RIVER TRAFFIC

Sailing barges of old frequented the wharf at The Spots and served local manufacturing and farming needs. There was a Quaker burial plot at The Spots until 1938.The Society of Friends acquired the burial ground in 1674 from Thomas Banks, a tailor, for 50 shillings on a 1,000 years' lease.

Market Cross via River Lane to the wharf is shown on the 1845 tithe map. Courtesy ESRO.

The Cuckmere bears nominal leisure traffic these days, like these canoeists about to make maximum use of the tides.

2. *The thoroughfare*

The Grade II listed Manor House.

BATS WING

This chalet may be recalled trading in various guises over the years, a saddlers, wool shop and novelties. In late 2003 it became The Trug Shop, carrying on a traditional craft from Herstmonceux. Sadly the business closed in November 2005.

The property is recorded being re-assembled in Alfriston as a leather workshop, after being one of a pair of cabbies' shelters at Victoria Station over a century ago.

NORTH STREET

This rare 1894 Ellis Kelsey view records North Street, with Rose Cottage central down the road. The area was known as 'down the bricks' as it led past riverside pastures that were used briefly as brick fields. In 1371 the Chichester Cathedral charters showed the thoroughfare being known as Bynorthstrete.

Looking up North Street from Rose Cottage, the neat row of terraced homes were built in the mid-1920s.

FORMER WORKHOUSE

In the early 1800s Nos 9 and 10 North Street were linked by internal doors as the village Union Poor House, that had been at Market Cross House. After the 1830s paupers detained therein were moved to Eastbourne Workhouse.

Charles (Bob) Hall the last member of the smuggling associates of Stanton Collins died aged 95 years in the Eastbourne Institution (workhouse) in 1895.

In 1801 a group of Dissenters broke away from St Andrew's and held meetings for a while in the terraced property No 13 High Street. It had been the village bakery run by Mr Harriott. Today it may be remembered as The Urn tea rooms, until 1960. In recent years it has been better known as Badgers Restaurant.

WATERLOO SUNSET

Alfriston's Grade I listed Market Cross in Waterloo Square is now but one of two extant examples. The cross was to remind traders that they were bound to deal honestly. The rival elaborate cross at Chichester remains intact, compared with the Alfriston cross that was re-created with a cornice stone on top in 1833.

The original Alfriston stone cross was erected in 1418 when King Henry IV permitted a market every Tuesday and two annual fairs on the feasts of Saint Andrew (November 29th), Saints Philip and James (April 30th).

The north side terrace was requisitioned as Quartermasters stores and billets known as Wellington Barracks for Napoleonic War troops. On April 18th 1917 the Officer Commanding, Seaford Camp, was sent a request from Alfriston parish council saying they were considerate of troops taking their leisure, but could they be better supervised. A Canadian soldier had been seen trying to climb the Market Cross and caused it to collapse, the trooper sustaining serious head injuries. The Army made the village out of bounds to its troops, a point that local traders promptly reacted to in fear of losing commerce.

November 1955: a lorry crashed into the cross shattering its shaft. Today's Market Cross is a replica topped by the carving of a shepherd's crown in the form of a sea urchin as carried by downland shepherds for good luck.

The cross was fortunate to remain intact after the July 2004 motorist's intrusion when Ye Olde Smugglers Inne was severely damaged.

Mrs Muddle (Turrell), Mrs Piper, unknown, Sid Selvey and Cecil Piper survey the wrecked Market Cross.

CHANGING PLACES

We found this confusing scene in an old book bearing the caption . . . The Old Smugglers Inn, now demolished, photographed in 1926.

A prompt response from Ron Levett identified the building as being part of the current Waterloo Square retail properties, as seen below.
   In the early 1800's manorial court books this whole block was called The Cross House. There is a 1753 link with John Mittell, a Brenchley mercer.

WATERLOO SQUARE

Village life recorded in autumn 1896 by Ellis Kelsey during a less hectic period for the parish. To this day Queen Victoria's coronation chestnut tree dominates the thoroughfare.

Nowhere has a sketch of the actual cross been found. The shaft was but a stub by 1780 and a new sea urchin cornice was installed in September 1833, the shaft being partially fabricated from surplus mullion windows at St Andrew's.

In the early 1800s troops were billeted around Alfriston and Winton Street amid the Napoleonic Wars. The victorious association with the Battle of Waterloo has been perpetuated.

CROSS HOUSE

Not Just Chocolates proprietor Geoff O'Brien took over the former Wood's butchers shop in 2004 and he enjoys life amid the village centre bustle. The clock was installed to commemorate Queen Elizabeth II's silver jubilee in 1977.

In the spring of 2006 it was planned to open a tourist information centre at the back of the shop.

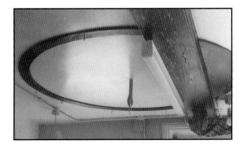

The Georgian block was built for the Elphick family in the mid-1800s, being occupied by a Mr Taylor as a general shop. It occupies the site of the former glove factory. Cross House has traded as Henry Pierce's carrier business and retains many features from its time as Woods butchers shop.

VILLAGE STORES

The Grade I listed bow windows date from the time entrepreneur Ebenezer Comfort occupied the Village Stores & Post Office. Len Wilde is remembered by many running the store from the 1930s to the 1950s and the property remains a focal point. The corner shop, seen left, in Rope Walk was a manse that became the first police station in 1840, with Constable No 6 Robert Baker.

In February 2006 new occupiers Ron and Bev Lion, with Bev's mother Anne Holmes, took over the central store from Barbara, Brian and Clare Rapson.

Fortunately subsequent owners have resisted the temptation to re-furbish the shop's interior fittings. Today the antique wooden shelving ambience is a prime asset of the business.

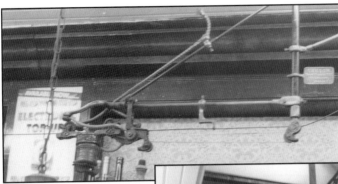

VICTORIAN TIMES

Novel features inside the Village Stores include this neat overhead Lamson mechanism for paying-in accounts. However, this antique was not used in this small shop and came from a larger store.

An item of intrigue is the old gallery where clients could examine an array of supplies stocked at the emporium.

The new owners are said to want to reinstate the divided stairway to the gallery that was last used as a GPO sorting office.

THE SMALLEST BANK

This building opposite Market Cross was built by John Wilson so that villagers had a local bank.

The branch opened twice a week and Mrs Stepney is recalled as a recent teller. The little building operated as Barclays Bank from September 1907 until April 1992 when they closed the facility.

The property is also called Bats Wing and has for some years now traded as The Apothecary.

SADDLERS HOUSE

Saddlers House, to the right of Star Inn, is pictured in the 1950s when petrol was served in the High Street from a hand operated pump - it is said the fuel tanks remain underground there. The store was run by a Mr Larkin and then former village policeman Edmund Purseglove and his wife who sold confectionery.

Herding cattle along the High Street may have been a familiar sight in 1894 when Ellis Kelsey took this photo. Such activity would cause an uproar now.

TWYTTON HOUSE

In the 1800s this now Grade II listed property was known as The Old Paint Shoppe and Tilly's Paint Shop, part of the self-contained community emanating around Alfriston's commercial centre.

It was more recently occupied by Radford's Antiques, but the house was sold during 2004 and has now been substantially refurbished. By November 2005 the shop premises re-opened as Chevan hairdressing salon.

The exterior walls bear several interesting time-pieces. A foundation stone a few inches above ground level in the alley bears JEE 1716, whilst another under the eaves states SEE 1733, after the locally-prominent Elphick family that built the house.

Of curio value are the pair of Guardian Insurance Company firemark plaques, indicating which premises the local horse-drawn fire service should attend to first.

Twytton House is described in the manorial court book of 1742 as a house, garden and backside in Alfriston, occupied by John Elphick. Similarly in 1750 the occupant was John Birchett and variously over the ensuing century ownership passed on between members of the family of Charles Springett Brooker and his son-in-law George Woodhams, the grocer.

A twiten is recognised as a Sussex term for an alleyway, lane or passage, between buildings.

LITERARY CENTRE

Towards the close of 2003 the former Magpie premises in the High Street were acquired by Cate Olson and Nash Robbins.

The couple had recently arrived in the UK from Boston, Massachusetts where they had been in the high quality book business for many years.

Since their creation of Much Ado Books they have established a new chapter - re-generating Alfriston as a literary and academic landmark.

MOONRAKERS

This High Street property is Grade II listed and was previously two homes, one occupied by members of the Lower family and the other abode by a Miss Olive. As one house it was called Two Ways and supposedly has been a wig makers workshop.

In the 1843 tithe award the block is listed as three houses, garden and yard of 0.16875 acres. It was then owned by Charles Springett Brooker and William Tucknott was the tenant. In 1926 Ron Levett was born in one of the cottages.

More recently as a restaurant it has traded as The Spinning Wheel, Wheelers and lastly as Moonrakers. In August 2005 Fleurets estate agents advertised the restaurant, that had been closed for some months, at a quarter off the former sale figure.

It was commented upon in 2005, when the Wingrove sought planning options, that the parish has ample refreshment facilities and that public trends change with the times, parking facilities having become an insurmountable problem for some traders.

The name Moonrakers arises from a Wiltshire legend of smugglers caught by Excise men while retrieving kegs of brandy hidden in a pond. They claimed to be simple-mindedly raking up the reflection of the moon.

Planning applications were lodged in mid-2006 for change of use for Moonrakers Restaurant to a class C3 dwelling house.

The maze of Sussex style tile-hung property and gables backing onto the Tye that were used as Harry Batho's racing stables. The five cottages date from the 1800s when Richard Porter built them and have long since been modernised as residential units.

The front of the former stable block, facing the narrow High Street, adds to the character of the village.

DEANS PLACE ESTATE

Records indicate that the Dene family owned local estates in Elizabethan times, the name being noted back to the mid-14th century. Their land extended over much of modern times Alfriston. However, from the 1700s ownership of Deans Place passed into other hands and the estate was largely divided up by auction at the White Hart in Lewes on December 20th 1891.

Mr Luff, landlord of the White Hart, catered for his fifty-odd guests amply before the auction. At the rostrum Alfred Baker, of the London company of solicitors, was able to find a purchaser for all the Lots - the sale being practically without reserve. The first portion of the estate consisted of fifty-five lots of freehold building sites, suitable for the erection of bungalows or small villas, plus a range of buildings suitable for dairy purposes being catalogued.

Lot 1 was a corner position of freehold building land. Alderman Farncombe secured this plot for £60, with a 308ft frontage to Kings Ride.

Lot 2, frontage 100ft by 189ft deep, also went to Mr Farncombe - at £30. Lots 3 to 6 fetched between £18-£30 to Messrs Champion, Cattermole and Wood. Lot 7, a corner plot of 100ft frontage and 230ft depth at the Broadway, was secured by Major Russel of Brighton for £16.

Mr Aucock bought Lot 9, of 110ft by 220ft, for £13. Lot 23, a range of brick and stone buildings, barns, outbuildings etc, close to the Vicarage was knocked down to Mr J.S. Ade for £115.

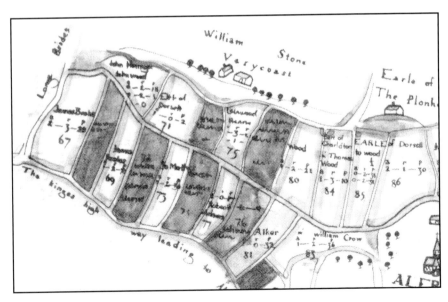

Medieval period maps show irregular parcels of land allocated in strips known as furlongs, each relative to features of the terrain. A furlong generally measures 220 yards by 20 yards. This association has been perpetuated in a local street name. This scene is de Warde's map of 1618 showing the river pastures.

FROG FIRLE

In the latter half of the 19th century Frog Firle was the home of Mr Austen Leigh who farmed the surrounding 550 acres with his brother. Their aunt Caroline kept house for them, and in 1867 wrote her memoir *My Aunt Jane Austen*, fifty years after the novelist's death. The house passed to the Youth Hostel Association in part lieu of death duties.

A bequest by Miss Caroline to St Andrew's parish church enabled the small south porch to be restored as an extra room which was itself updated in 1999 as part of St Andrew's Millennium project.

In early 2005 traffic calming outside Frog Firle was undertaken by narrowing the highway to single lane traffic.

BURNT HOUSE

The gaunt and statuesque home alongside the White Way road, southerly to High and Over and Seaford, was once part of a much larger mansion.

It was originally built by Thomas Chowne in the early 1600s as part of Place House. In June 1765, whilst Mr Chowne's great-great-grandson resided there, a raging fire in the library destroyed the majority of the mansion. These remains became known locally as Burnt House. The farm alone covered 443 acres.

3. *Hostelries*

The Wingrove c1890.

PUBLIC HOUSES - THEN AND NOW

The Star Inn is noted for its ornate facia carvings, one is of St George slaying the Dragon. The inn was redecorated in its current imposing colours during 1968-1969. In mid-july 2006 the privately owned hotel was surprisingly put on the market valued at £2.2m. This follows a curious trend in High Street premises in just over a year when The Village Stores & Post Office, Trug Shop, Moonrakers, Wingrove Hotel, Grizzly Business, Hike & Bike and, latterly, The Gallery came on the market.

Ye Olde Smugglers Inne, seen in early 2004, had changed little during centuries of local strife - until that July when an errant driver intruded upon its hospitality.

STAR INN

The hostelry is recorded above in 1896 by Ellis Kelsey whilst the frontage was rendered to protect the timber frame. The stucco was removed in 1902 to treat the woodwork. The name has been spelt out as Starre. The Horsham Stone roof slabs are said to each weigh about 2 tons. The cut-away at this end of Star Lane, where the lion carving stood, was to allow for a bottle and jug facility. The hostelry dates from 1520 when it was built by the Bishop of Battle. The inn had leisurely retreat associations, as a stop-over for a variety of travellers.

This Wrench Series postcard shows a tranquil High Street in about 1900. The road is metalled and kerbs are in place. Perhaps Alfriston is the perfect place for a literal pub crawl with a choice of five inns to frequent!

THE LANDMARK MARKET CROSS INN

In the early 1820s rebellious Stanton Collins ran Market House as a butchers shop and it became a haunt for his smuggling activities. Church wardens were tenants between 1827-1831 when Market Cross House was run as an almshouse for parish paupers. (ESRO 5681/51/1-10 deeds of Market Cross House). Possibly this relates to part of the property.

When motorists and tourism re-invented Alfriston from the early 1920s the whole property became Ye Olde Smugglers Inn.

THE GEORGE INN

Dating from the 14th century as licensed premises the George & Dragon was a notable coaching inn. The vast Wealden hall frame has accommodated varying trades under its roof - barbers, butchers, a garage and a coach-house.

The tile-hung premises, seen below in the 1930s, were rebuilt with the medieval timber frontage after a fire in 1943 destroyed most of the Horsham Stone roof; remnants can be seen along the eaves.

The fire was discovered in a small ground floor bar just after 3.00am on Sunday 30th November by licensee Mr Faulkner. Eastbourne firemen and two NFS men extinguished the inferno by 5.30am - stopping it spreading to adjoining buildings. There is a local story that two firemen would not attend the fire until they went home and got their uniforms on!

A nearby Army ammunition dump could have devastated the village had the wind been blowing another way.

THE WINGROVE

The imposing colonial-style Wingrove Inn was built as a home in 1870 for race-horse trainer Richard Porter, the verandah being an addition. It is said that Mr Porter lost his assets when he stood surety for a friend's debts. Leading trainer Harry Batho arrived in Alfriston in 1898 and leased the then empty Wingrove.

Harry Batho built a new house in Sloe Lane called Wargrave in 1914, that eventually became the White Lodge Country House Hotel. Batho bought back Wingrove with its vital 200-acre local estate from James White in mid-1920, but tragically Batho suffered a massive stroke and died four months later in September 1925 aged just 55 years. He is buried at St Andrew's.

In the early 1970s the hotel traded as Chateau Anglais, before reverting to the Wingrove. Mel and Susan Butcher had brought the site in 2000 and then during 2004 they announced plans to retire. Developers intended to extend the property and convert it into five apartments, but GM Associates were refused planning permission. In November 2005 ownership passed on to Sussex wine merchant and restaurateurs David and Carri Allcorn. May 2006: the Wingrove re-opened after extensive alterations. The new bar from June 9th and a 60-cover restaurant opened the following week. It is now Wingrove House.

STEAMER INN

The former Steamer Inn premises are another fine example of a local Wealden hall, although it has been variously altered over the centuries.

No mention of the name origins has been forthcoming. Steaming might apply to animal skins - curing - tanning - action of steam - cook by steam.

There is a link from 1753-1781 in the ownership of John Batchelor, possibly as the Mercers Arms. His guardian was John Mittell, a Kent mercer - a mercer being a trader in textile fabrics, especially silks.

In the 1890s the corner site became Bodle's Dairy, then in the 1920s a well-known local family named Hilton occupied the second cottage, it was still open to the roof and had wooden seats around the room. The shop was occupied in the early 1950s by Cecil Holt, a greengrocer. Liz and David Phillips started their Steamer Trading Cookshop chain of six kitchenware outlets there in 1986.

DEANS PLACE

For many years the hotel complex has been a popular and thriving tourist retreat, with high levels of service and quality run by the Best Western Group.

In the past the property had been a private home, a farmhouse, a hydro resort, an isolation hospital - and even the local pest house.

In February 2006 Deans Place hosted a local audience and the Harry Strutters Hot Rhythm Orchestra as a Charter 600 promotional function. The entertainer Jim Heath is seen providing a lively vocal refrain.

WHITE LODGE HOTEL

This imposing colonial style villa was built in 1915 as Wargrave, a private home for Harry Batho. The Sloe Lane property was named after a famous race-horse he trained for the unfortunate rogue Horatio Bottomley MP.

In the 1950s it was developed as a hotel by Mr & Mrs Denyer, subsequently Hydro Hotel acquired the site in early 2003. However, the hotel was set to close in September 2005 after being acquired for £1.7m by Oakdene Homes plc which launched its plans to convert the five acre complex around 13 two-bedroomed private apartments.

INCIDENT AT THE MARKET CROSS

After a superb summer's evening talk by Johnnie Johnson on Sussex Crimes and Criminals most of us went home quite contented.

Around 3.00am next morning, July 14th 2004, landlord Robert Scott and his wife Maureen had a serious crime case inflicted on their premises.

An errant driver had struck the Market Cross plinth and ricocheted into the public house, demolishing the Tudor exterior wall. The car reversed from the bar and sped away, leaving the parish with a most unlikely tourist attraction.

Remarkably there were no injuries.

Having stood
since the 14ᵗʰ century
Ye Olde Smugglers Inne
(formerly The Market Inn)
was the victim of a hit & run crash
in the early hours of 14ᵗʰ July 2004
Amazingly, Maureen Scott, Landlady
of 27 years, and her husband Rob, slept
through the incident ~ to be woken by
firemen and police!

AS SHOWN THE DAMAGE WAS EXTENSIVE
& RESTORATION COULD TAKE 6 MONTHS

The landlord quipped that he would hang a sign stating Robbie's Drive-In Bar - get smashed any time day or night - on what remained of the façade.

Later that month Seaford artist Abigail Barker created a series of amusing murals, depicting the intrusion, on the hoardings erected whilst reconstruction took place. Just over a year later the hoardings were removed.

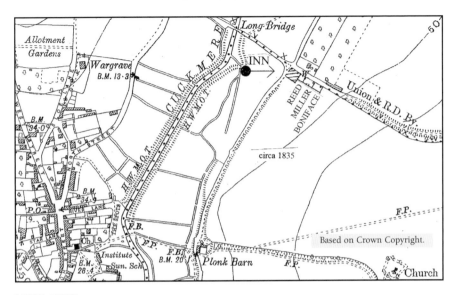

circa 1835

Based on Crown Copyright.

LOST INNS

The location of the Royal Oak site has been determined from tithes at a corner of a field at Peachey's Corner. The premises had become a house of ill-repute when last recorded during a period of frugal social standards locally.

It is described in 1698 as a little cottage lately built on waste at Four Wents on the Long Bridge to Eastbourne Road. By 1791 it is noted as messuage called the Royal Oak. Shown in 1831 and 1845 as a public house and three cottages, but the 1861 census shows no buildings at all.

Peachey's Lane (below) is part of the intriguing Glyndebridge turnpike under the Downs from Lewes via Glynde to Winton Street, over Long Bridge, across Windover Hill and on to Jevington/Polegate and Eastbourne.

No confirmed site has been found for the Mercers Arms, Alfriston, that was recorded circa 1650-1700 run by William Chitendin. The Royal Oak at Milton Street was re-named the Sussex Ox in 1972 after its acquisition by Charringtons.

Site of the 1800s Royal Oak Inn.

4. *Personalities*

ESRO Senior Archivist Christopher Whittick
opened the Charter 600 event with a reading
from the charter in the original Latin.

CAPTAIN DOUGLAS ANN

Any synopsis of the lower Cuckmere regions would be incomplete without acknowledging the role of Captain Louis Douglas Ann MBE for his lasting contribution towards appreciation of the district.

Douglas Ann moved to the area with his family as a boy and went to school in Eastbourne. During the Great War he served overseas and in Palestine sustained shrapnel injuries to his left leg that left him with a distinct limp for the rest of his life. On his return to civilian life Douglas Ann acquired the Old Thatch at Hellingly and specialised in breeding pedigree poultry. They also took in farming students.

In 1923 Douglas, and his first wife Drusilla, were attracted to the potential of a derelict bone mill site at Lower Berwick. Up to WWI the premises processed bone for glue and fertilisers. Importantly Douglas Ann bought the site and 25 acres of land southward off the A27 highway. Towards the close of the 1920s Drusillas Tea Gardens had a glowing reputation as a fashionable gathering place. The car park was described in promotional literature as the Motor Show of the South - adding to the popular Restaurant, Miniature Railway and growing Zoo and Cuckmere punting attractions.

An interesting landmark is the Golden Galleon at Exceat opened by Captain Ann as Tea Rooms in 1930. Michael Ann recalls that the name Golden Galleon is thought to have been coined by one of the young lady students at the Tea Rooms Finishing School who likened the location to its golden setting, with galleon being a logical coastal literation.

Captain Ann sold the Golden Galleon as an empty building in 1946 when troops vacated the premises. As a WWII serving soldier Captain Ann became Adjutant of the local Home Guard, while his second wife Elizabeth operated the Tea Gardens complex. Captain Ann was awarded the MBE in the latter stages of WWII as he returned to re-build Drusillas Zoo, with its gardens and railway.

A disastrous fire at their Thatched Barn office in 1953 destroyed many family records. After Captain Ann passed away in 1958 the enterprise was carried on by his son Michael Ann, joined later by his younger brother Christopher (known as Topper by his contemporaries) who set up the neighbouring English Wine Centre.

In the January 1998 New Year Honours List Michael Ann was awarded the OBE for services to the young and South East tourism. Both Michael and Christopher have now opted for a retirement role, but enthusiastically participate in area activities.

In early May 1997 it was announced that the long-standing Drusillas Park family business had been sold to Laurence and Christine Smith. They proposed to maintain the zoo, with its 90 species on show, and the restaurant complex in the entertaining and educational style created by Douglas Ann 74 years previously.

In late March 2006 the *Sussex Express* reported . . . It's business as usual at Alfriston's English Wine Centre after news that the site could be taken over by a local charity. The centre has received calls from clients asking if it will close and be put on the market. Wine Centre founder and owner Christopher Ann assured people - including those who had booked weddings - that the business would be sold as a going concern. It would run side by side with any future change of use of accommodation on site. Chef Steve Mitchell holds a three-year franchise to run the centre's catering and would be unaffected by any outcome of the business sale. Wealden District Council had an outline planning application to turn the centre into providing services for adults with learning difficulties. Christopher said . . . There comes a stage when we have to plan for our retirement, but the Wine Centre will be delivering business as usual.

Onward Drusillas devotees

In February 2006 all 90 Alfriston School pupils were invited to pay a visit to Drusillas to deliver their verdict on £500,000 worth of new play equipment at the amusement park. The childrens' task was to try the latest attraction called Amazon Park. The equipment consists of soft-play shapes, jumbo slides, netted walkways, spinning poles along with varied jumping, climbing and crawling apparatus. There is also a segregated area for under six-year-olds. Owner Laurence Smith said the visit from Alfriston School would enable them to see how the 300sqm attraction would operate, providing a foresight into any problems before they open to the public.

JAMES BATHO

The name of James Harold Batho was synonymous with racing at Alfriston from his acquisition of Wingrove in 1898 until his untimely death there in 1925.

Batho (JHB) had established an impressive list of clientele, training horses for royalty and celebrities. One such personage was Horatio William Bottomley, the rogue MP based at The Dicker. Two of Bottomley's horses trained by JHB did exceptionally well. *Le Blizon* won the Batthyany Plate in 1899 and 1900 and the Prix de la Manche in 1901, 1902 and 1903. *Wargrave* won five races as a four-year-old in 1902 and the Ebor Handicap and Cesarewitch in 1904. When *Long Set* won the Lincoln JHB purchased an ox from Woods butchers shop and it was chopped up and laid out on trestles on the Tye for villagers.

Batho chose to build a family home on land acquired at Sloefields. He did so in 1914 and he named the property Wargrave after the successful racehorse and after his wife declared that the footings needed to be extended to make a bigger house. They moved in during the summer of 1915 - the house later became known as White Lodge Hotel (page 43).

Wingrove stood empty from this time until in July 1920 when JHB bought back Wingrove and its associated lands from the then owner James White. This return was to stop any other trainers securing access to the training gallops and assets like the 200 acres that made up the Wingrove estate, including eight acres fronting Kings Ride. The largest parcel of land was 187 acres of downland encompassing France Bottom and Short Bottom with their gallops - plus land to the west of The Broadway from Kings Ride to Uplands. He planted a wood behind The Broadway as cover for his pheasants.

Bottomley had paid for the construction of a billiard room at Wingrove as a reward for JHB's racing prowess. It was perhaps ironic that James Batho spent his last four months in the billiard room, unable to be moved, after suffering a major stroke there in June 1925.

The billiard room became the main bar at the Wingrove.

Batho's daughter Evelyn had acted as his deputy trainer since 1916 until his demise and was an expert and very knowledgeable horsewoman. However at the time, the Jockey Club would not allow women to hold a trainer's licence and Wingrove was sold to Lord Queenborough who was looking for somewhere to install his own trainer.

James Batho's benevolence ranged from sharing his purse with numerous social activities. He was President of the Cuckmere Valley Cricket League. He was also an ardent supporter of the Boy Scouts movement, contributing largely to the local troop funds.

DENIS HEALEY

There is something perhaps essentially English that a well-known personality, a celebrity, can walk around their home neighbourhood and pass without a fuss, perhaps with just a polite acknowledgment. In fact Denis Healey has lived near Alfriston for over 25 years and is well past the incomer category.

The Right Honourable Lord Denis Healey CH MBE was born in 1917 at Keighley, Yorkshire, the son of an engineer. When he was eight years old he won a scholarship to Bradford Grammar School.

In 1936 he entered Balliol College, Oxford and became active in politics. On the outbreak of WWII he joined the British Army and served with the Royal Engineers in North Africa, Sicily and Italy. This included being Military Landing Officer to the British assault brigade for Anzio. He had joined the Labour Party and in the 1945 General Election stood for Pudsey and Otley.

In 1952 Denis Healey was elected to the House of Commons. On the right of the party Healey became an outspoken critic of prominent Aneurin Bevan and his loyal followers. In 1959 Hugh Gaitskell appointed Healey to the Shadow Cabinet.

When the Labour Party was elected in the 1964 General Election Harold Wilson, the new prime minister, appointed Denis Healey as his Secretary of State for Defence. He held the post until the defeat of the Labour government in the 1970 General Election. Subsequently, in 1974, Harold Wilson appointed Healey as Chancellor of the Exchequer. When Wilson resigned in 1976, Healey stood for the leadership but was defeated by James Callaghan.

In 1980 Healey once again contested the leadership of the Labour Party. He was unexpectedly defeated by Michael Foot and accepted the post of deputy leader. Denis Healey resigned from the Shadow Cabinet in 1987. In more recent years Lord and Lady Healey have enjoyed their retirement in recreations, and as welcome participants in numerous local activities.

His autobiography, *The Time of My Life*, was published in 1989. Lady Healey launched her autobiography, *Part of the Pattern* in March 2006, via Much Ado.

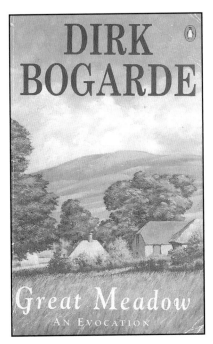

SIR DIRK BOGARDE (1921-1999)

As a boy (in his real name of Derek Niven van den Bogaerde) he spent several idyllic summer holidays at Lullington in company with his younger sister Elizabeth and Lally their nanny.

In his Penguin titles *A Postillion Struck by Lightning* and *Great Meadow* he recalls their adventures and characters in and around Alfriston.

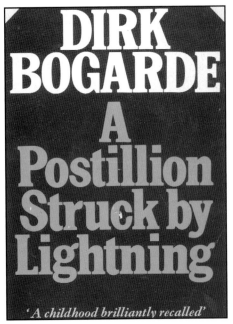

REMEMBERING SID DUMBRELL

An endearing spectacle of the cortege of friends and family of Sidney Dumbrell, who passed away December 2nd 2005, was the procession led by his Jack Russell terrier Scamp - as they moved from the Broadway down to the United Reformed Church.

Sid Dumbrell had lived nearly all his 91 years in Alfriston, being born in Milton Street in 1914. He is remembered as a countryman, a gardener and game-keeper and local character. Some recall him as a member of the Abbots Wood patrol of the secret rearguard Home Guard with a hideout in Folkington Wood.

ROYAL PATRONAGE

Queen Mary is seen above leaving The Star after lunch in 1935. Her Majesty had been to see King George V who had been resting at Compton Place, Eastbourne - the home of the Duke of Devonshire.

The visit of King George and Queen Mary to the area, during February and March 1935, is well recorded. On Saturday March 16th the King and Queen drove to the Wish Tower, walking to Holywell along the lower parade.

King George and Queen Mary used chalet No 2 at Holywell - returning to London on Tuesday 26th March. King George V died the following year and their controversial son Edward inherited the throne - and years of furore ensued over the enigmatic monarchy.

A LOVELY LADY

The close of 2005 sadly marked the passing of Clara Muddle at the grand age of 102 years.

Clara had been born in Selmeston and lived all her married life in Lullington and then Alfriston, sharing the years of change locally.

After leaving her cottage Clara moved into care at Abbeyfield and spent her last months at Threeways Home in Seaford.

DICK WAKEHAM

Another link with the parish past was lost with the passing of Richard Wakeham in early February 2006.

He was known to everybody as Dick and was a much-loved and familiar character around the village. His working life was linked to market gardens at the Willows by the river.

His funeral service was at St Andrew's Church on Monday 27th February.

THE LEVETTS OF ALFRISTON

Ron Levett comes from an old Alfriston family that can trace their line back to 1613. Ron was born in 1926 in one of the High Street cottages that eventually became Moonrakers Restaurant. His grandmother Ellen Comfort was a relative of Ebenezer Comfort who ran the village store opposite the Market Cross for many years. The Levett surname is found in neighbourhoods around Alfriston.

Ron's father had been bequeathed some money, in the early 1930s, by Ellen and he purchased a piece of land alongside the end of The Furlongs on which to build. The chalet home came as a kind of timberwork kit to be clad with asbestos sheeting. The growing family subsequently moved into other village houses.

On his return in 1948 from WWII duty with the Royal Scots Greys, as a wireless operator on tanks, Ron developed his army training with radios and the partnership that became Norvett Electronics Ltd has served the rural district from that time.

Amongst his local interests Ron is a keen member of Alfriston & District Royal British Legion.

He has lengthy recollections of growing up around Alfriston via his website. Ron's memorabilia is going into book format to add to the parish archives.
www.alfristonline.co.uk

THE TREADLE DENTIST AND DRUNKEN CHICKENS

Michael T. H. Clark has an innate affinity with Alfriston through family links. His great-grandfather was Henry Robert Browne. In 1860 he established a pharmacy in Cornfield Road, Eastbourne, and many of his clients were from Alfriston's horse-racing community who came to him for horse balls. The association was extended when his great-grandfather purchased Foller's Manor adjacent to Frog Firle.

In September 1940 Michael, then a schoolboy, moved with his parents to Alfriston to avoid the pressures of WWII. In those days there was no electricity or gas in the village. Lighting was provided by oil lamps and cooking was by means of oil stoves. Heating was by open fires or a paraffin stove.

On one occasion Michael had to see Mr Visick, his dentist, who had moved his practice from Eastbourne to Peachey's Corner. The lack of electricity brought varied problems and Mr Visick's drill was operated by foot treadle. The quality of light by oil lamp was poor, which made it impossible for a dentist to function adequately. Michael adds these factors undoubtedly contributed to his patient's discomfort.

Many of Alfriston's commercial outlets were in transition, one was the rope-making works site that became an orchard. This enterprise also ebbed and became a chicken run. At the close of each September the windfalls fermented, providing an alcoholic banquet for the hens. They staggered around in drunken ecstasy, their inebriated cluckings giving rise to a sequence of cacophonous crescendos. The inebriated birds were a source of great amusement for the village youngsters.

ALFRISTON'S FIRST DIARIST

For many years Florence Pagden's title *History of Alfriston* was regarded as the definitive work on the village. First published by Combridges, of Church Road, Hove in 1895 the book ran to ten editions up to 1950 and was indeed a handy pocket book. Copies are still available from specialist booksellers and its content must be viewed as non-questionable, although fuller accounts and other local studies have ensued in the on-going 50 years.

In some ways the booklet can be frustrating in that it does not go into any greater details on some topics, when the writer had access to invaluable material at the time. Such information, personal recollections and anecdotes, can be the substance of such books and Alfriston is indeed rich in its past and with a ready supply of visitors hungry for nostalgia.

The Pagden family had strong local connections for centuries and Florence became Mrs Hubert Winstanley. She wrote of the changes locally from the 1900s and she featured in numerous local societies herself. It is said she held the village together at the time with her connections and social rounds. In those times local life was simple, almost feudal. Her book is available in ESCC library systems and is well worth a read.

JOSEPH DUMBRELL'S FAMILY

Mrs Evelyn Vines, nee Dumbrell, was one of eight children born to Joseph Dumbrell. Evelyn was born in 1914 and has lived in Alfriston all her life and has a wealth of memories to relate. Her father Joseph was landlord at The George and kept his fly carriage garaged in the southern end of the inn. Joseph Dumbrell passed on aged 79 years in 1956.

Evelyn met her future husband, Albert, out one Sunday with friends on Eastbourne seafront, whilst he was employed on construction work at the bridge at Polegate. The couple had two daughters and Albert enrolled in the Army in 1939. Gunner Vines of the Royal Artillery lost his life in Italy in September 1944 and is one of the six WWII Servicemen commemorated in St Andrew's Church. Evelyn became a village Post Office delivery person.

The pre-war years are a particular period of interest and Evelyn has been able to identify many of the characters portrayed in Dirk Bogarde's memoirs. As youngsters they too would play hide-and-seek around the sunken road from Plonk Barn to Lullington Church that was known as the Little Chapel. Children would tease caravan dweller Mrs Bristow - aka Nellie Wardle.

THE GHOST WALK

Michael T.H. Clark recalls that his relatives Walter and Ethel Comfort of Greyholm created what they called the Ghost Walk. It ran from the garden along the lower slopes of a hill and consisted mainly of thick blackthorn shrubs (sloes) through which they cut a tunnel, with the shrubs meeting overhead.

Some cases of these features were said to be the 'holloways' of Sussex. At the end of the tunnel the walk continued over downland which eventually lead to Comfort's Bottom.

AROUND THE PARISH

The Rev Frank Fox-Wilson BTh joined the Alfriston environs in 1993 when he became Rector at St Andrew's.

Amongst varied projects at his previous parish he had compiled a community record entitled *The Story of Goring and Highdown* to add to county archives. His year 2000 book *Carving Nature* runs to 192pp and became an invaluable addition to the library of woodcarvers, who love carving nature and wildlife. There is lots of advice on tools and techniques, along with projects for novice readers to immerse themselves in. Then in 2002 he undertook restoration of Alfriston's lion figurehead resident, much to the delight of local people and visitors to the village.

According to a recent *Cuckmere News* report the Rector's first professional job was as a jazz guitarist and at times now he lets loose on jazz drums.

The Rev Michael Loughton and his wife Liz have been involved with the Cuckmere parishes for some 25 years. Michael has particular connections with Litlington Church, but also helps regularly throughout the benefice. They used to live at Follers Manor before moving to Seaford.

The Rev Ian Hunter and his wife Peggy live at Seaford and have been part of St Andrew's congregation for several years. Ian assists by taking some weekday and Sunday Services as holiday cover etc. He was ordained as a Deacon in 1943.

The Rev Mary Stilwell retired recently as Chaplain and Head of Religious Education at Roedean School. Her husband Isla is Musical Director of Seaford Silver Band. Mary is ordained as a Deacon and is thus licensed to preach and take on many functions normally carried out by a priest. They live in Seaford.

The Rev Canon John Lloyd-James also lives at Seaford and before retirement was the Vicar of Bishopstone. John helps out at Alfriston mainly on Sundays. His previous ministry included eight years at St Mary's, Kemp Town, Brighton.

The Rev Dr Gerald Munro is Minister at Alfriston United Reformed Church, along with responsibilities at the Seaford and Eastbourne's Upperton Road United Reformed churches. Gerald and his wife Janice live in Seaford and Gerald has become a familiar face each month at St Andrew's.

At St Andrew's one of the recent issues, from the start of 2004, has been closer unity with the United Reformed Church.

The previous year discussions had been going on to think the unthinkable - one congregation.

The full unity of St Andrew's and the United Reformed Church took place on April 9th 2006.

St Andrew's Day November 2004 was a double celebration. The Patronal Festival for St Andrew also marked the 60th anniversary of ordination of the Rev Ian Hunter.

The monthly publication *Cuckmere News* serves as a welcoming voice for views and news from Alfriston - along with communities at Lullington, Litlington and West Dean.

CATE OLSON AND NASH ROBBINS

The closure of smaller independent retail units in urban areas across the nation is an unfortunate yet significant statement of social and business trends. Alfriston's shops, however, have always been a sought-after commodity. The flow of tourists at large and local trade have readily adapted to the cycle of supply and consumer demand over the years. When the prime position that had been Magpie Gifts for many years became available this was one such Alfriston shop that was not going to be vacant for long.

Cate Olson and Nash Robbins are friends of Lynne Truss whose innovative and addictive work on punctuation - *Eats, Shoots, Leaves* - shot into the best-selling lists in 2003. (It was described as the zero tolerance guide.) It was from their friendship with Brighton resident Lynne that Cate and Nash learnt of the potential of the Magpie premises becoming available in Alfriston.

Nash has an enviable background in old, out-of-print and antiquarian titles - a compulsion that he has been able to build upon to become his vocation. His now familiar position around computers in their High Street store is the hub of an ever-expanding outlet into the world of books. Cate's charming manner and attractive Boston, USA accent extend their invitation to the bookshelves and the wealth of knowledge that have taken over the floor space at Much Ado Books.

One of the first changes made at their new shop was to open up the ground floor rooms, to realise fully the potential of the embryo business. The spoken word soon got around of the welcome being made to visitors and of the services coming on-stream at Much Ado Books.

Their entrepreneurial spirit, as they became established in Alfriston, has seen them organise a series of academic literary events with diverse international authors and celebrities being accessible to participants.

Complementing their on-going adventures into the world of literature in early 2006 Much Ado published the recollections of Lady Edna Healey titled *Part of the Pattern - memoirs of a wife at Westminster.*

Alfriston is indeed a much brighter place to be with the presence of Cate Olson and Nash Robbins at Much Ado Books.

shop@muchadobooks.com
www.muchadobooks.com

CHAMPIONS OF THE POOR

One of the outcomes of Octavia Hill's many social reforms was the foundation of the National Trust whose first acquisition was Alfriston's Clergy House. The vicar at the time, the Rev Mr Hodges, is said to have climbed upon a handy wheelbarrow to proclaim the news to the assembled villagers.

Under the inspiration of Christian Socialism Octavia Hill (1838-1912) and her sisters devoted their lives to the poor. They wrought miracles in slum houses by intelligent guidance, simple rules and sympathy.

JACK CADE'S REBELLION - 1450

Though this civil uprising is best commemorated in Heathfield, where it was claimed the fleeing leader was killed, more than 20 Alfriston men can be identified by name and occupation in the pardon granted by King Henry VI.

Among the list of local farmers, carpenters, smiths and others is one William atte Dene, whose ancestor appeared in Alfriston a century earlier living at the site of today's Deans Place.

HORATIO BOTTOMLEY

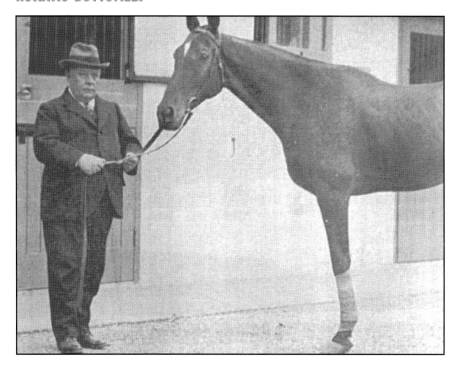

Horatio Bottomley gained his knowledge of the law through court room work as a self-taught shorthand writer. He became astute enough to conduct every one (except the very last) of his many legal cases. From his home at Upper Dicker Horatio - a man from humble beginnings - was seldom out of the headlines as a newspaper proprietor (he created *John Bull* magazine), an orator and champion of the poor, as a Member of Parliament and fraudster. He often visited Alfriston. He kept racehorses at the Wingrove stables of Harry Batho and netted £70,000 in wagers when his horse won the Cesarewitch. Bottomley celebrated by building the billiard room which later became the River Room Restaurant at the Wingrove Hotel.

He was bankrupt three times, his illicit dealings eventually earned him a seven year jail sentence. In 1932 he emerged to be engaged by the Windmill Theatre billed in *Revuedeville in Excelsis* - as a straight man (between showgirl acts) to humble his scandalous life.

He loved the Downs above Alfriston and four years after his death in 1933 (aged 73) his ashes were scattered there.

In October 2003 the Alfriston Players staged a memorable portrayal titled *Horatio* - perpetuating the role of the rogue MP and local characters of his time.

FAMILY CONNECTIONS

IN MEMORY OF

JOHN HARYOTT, BORN JULY 10.1819, DIED FEB.28.1877.
MARY, WIFE OF THE ABOVE, BORN JAN.18.1824, DIED MARCH.7.1906.
MARGARET, BORN APRIL 16.1858, DIED NOV. 4.1876.
MARY, BORN SEP. 8.1848, DIED JUNE 3.1892.
SUSANAH, BORN OCT. 8.1853, DIED AUG. 14.1894.
CATHERINE, BORN NOV. 3.1861, DIED FEB. 18.1900.
JOHN, BORN AUGUST 7. 1855, DIED MAY 2. 1905.
ARTHUR, BORN MAY 2. 1860, DIED JULY 31. 1932.
ANN, 1858 – 1934. AND **ALICE,** 1864 – 1920.
SUSANAH ALLWORK, BORN OCT. 25.1792, DIED OCT. 14.1871.
THY KINGDOM COME.

This memorial tablet in the south transept of Alfriston Church spans almost a century and a half. Susanah Allwork was born only six weeks after the birth of the French Republic, although the years for her birth and death above appear confused.

The descendant Ann Haryott died in 1906, the year the Soviet Union was admitted to the League of Nations. For many years from 1843 Richard Harriott and his descendants operated a bakery from premises in North Street now known as Badgers Restaurant.

CUCKMERE VALLEY LIGHT RAILWAY

On the back of the post-1850s era of railway expansions and potential a number of local dignatories, landowners, planners and legal experts devised a railway route from a siding at Berwick station to Birling Farm.

Had the railway been constructed and survived subsequent years of cut-backs by the 21st century it could have contributed to the local attractions. The 4-foot and 8.5-inch track was to have been laid in three stages. It was routed southeast by the river over Alfriston and Lullington pastures and bridges into Litlington and then to arc round to West Dean. The second section was to run to Friston Waterworks where a siding served the works there. The final section was to run across open ground terminating at Birling Farm.

In hindsight the track, banking, earthworks and yards - or their relics - would have cut severely into fields, scarring the countryside, although the instigators of the route might have cared little for any such considerations.

Plans and maps at The National Archive, Kew. MT 54/17 and MT 6/814/6.

5. *Faith and folklore*

Between August-December 2005 the Clergy House
underwent a £100,000 thatching renewal.

1896

CLERGY HOUSE

The 14th-century timber-framed Clergy House is worthy of a visit. It was the first building to be acquired by the National Trust, in 1896 for a peppercorn £10, but it was in a ruinous condition prior to further renovation in 1977. It nestles squat beside St Andrew's Church standing on its mound.

It may be noted that the Clergy House was not always used by the clergy. Many of the vicars were pluralists who resided outside of the parish and the house became occupied by farm labourers prior to acquisition by the Sussex Archaeological Society who bequeathed it to the embryo National Trust.

The house was re-thatched in 1939, then in late 2005 a £100,000 conservation schedule, that could be observed by the public, included a new wheat straw roof.

THE MYSTERY OF ST ANDREW'S EAST WINDOW

Generally it may be said that ecclesiastical records are accessible in an abundance, indeed far more so than those of parishioners going back several centuries. Yet St Andrew's Church, with its splendid ornate ambience, had kept a secret from the 1800s that was in view of the congregations. The creation of St Andrew's east window has recently been extensively researched by Peter Radford and Vernon Reynolds who have produced a 20pp booklet account of their findings that is available at the church.

In 2004 the pair of newcomers to Alfriston, who had not met previously, were kneeling in front of the altar. Vernon began to study the pair of dark memorial plaques towards the foot of the window. Lower left shows the window was erected in memory of Andrew Montagu, born 1853 and died 1884. The right side shows the window was dedicated by his brother Charles Wallace Montagu in 1904. For many years (till removal in 1987) the ornate reredos had concealed this information. Unravelling the mystery of the east window took the pair several months to determine and involved delving into dark Victorian family archives.

The stained-glass window was created by the eminent firm of James Powell & Co whose records are held in the Archive of Art and Design at the Victoria and Albert Museum.

FOLKLORE AND LEGENDS

A historic haunt like Alfriston needs little heed to create tales of old, the place abounds with secret passages, colourful characters and activities to consume countless hours - or indeed pages of a book.

Numerous social events are held on the Tye recreation ground, like this scene from August Bank Holiday 2005. Tye derives from the Saxon teag. The land was Crown property being part of the Duchy of Lancaster. However, in about 1880, it was presented to the parish by William Sanger.

BURLOW CASTLE

The fairies, it is said, used to dwell in the area, just to the north-east of Alfriston in a place called Burlow (or Burlough) Castle, a natural feature on the edge of the Downs above the Cuckmere. The top has been ploughed until nearly flat and a Paleolithic handaxe was found in the 19th century.

A theory suggests the area was also used as a medieval fort though it is now little more than a steep banked hillock topped by a meadow. There is an old story about two men who were ploughing the area and heard a fairy from below ground who said he had been baking and had broken his peel. One of the men mended it and was later rewarded with some fairy beer, but the other maintained there were no such things as fairies and wasted away. He died exactly a year later. There is very little written about the fort, though there are a few accounts of some stones from the original castle atop the mound.

Thomas Geering in *Our Sussex Parish* says that the last of the stones were taken for road making by a man called William Hills. Perhaps the fortification is Saxon as Burlow is a Saxon term for a defended place. The other earthwork just to the south is called The Rookery, a name more to do with recent residents than its original function as a possible Norman motte and bailey, though there was allegedly a 14th-century chapel on the site.

WITCHCRAFT

Accusations of bewitchment were levelled against Ursula Welfare of Alfriston in 1580. She was accused of bewitching 1 Sow, 8 Chickens and 2 Hens, though she was acquitted of the charges.

MONARCHS

It was said by a waitress at the Star Inn that a kitchen cauldron there was the one in which King Alfred burnt his cakes. The king was said to have given his name to the village of Alfriston, but this has now been disproved by early forms.

SHEPHERDS

An ancient funerary custom used up to the 1930s was the practice of burying a shepherd holding a small piece of fleece, so when he got to heaven St Peter could see he was a shepherd and forgive his lack of churchgoing due to the demands of his work. The custom died out when downland shepherds were eclipsed by the passage of time.

DOMESTIC DISPUTES

When a man and his wife were in severe disagreement, and the male was guilty of violence, then village women would lay chaff and straw by their front door to symbolise that a beating had taken place inside.

PARISH BEADLE

The imposing beadle with his long cape, coloured coat, and cocked hat trimmed in yellow would proclaim from the Market Cross, his long staff hammering in his hand. His superior attitude struck terror to small boys and also provoked admiration from older men.

WHITE HORSE OF LITLINGTON

Seen on the escarpment of High and Over is the large white horse carving that looks east over the Cuckmere acres.

There have been two white horses on the hill, the first lasting until the 1920s, cut in 1838 by James Pagden of Frog Firle Farm and his two brothers, to commemorate the coronation of Queen Victoria. Alternatively it was cut in 1860 by two youths who saw a patch of bare chalk in the turf that looked like a horse's head and they added the body.

The second horse visible now, and maintained in very good condition, was cut in 1924 by John T. Ade, Mr Bovis and Eric Hobbis. The trio cut the horse overnight with a full moon to see by, so as to startle the locals with the sudden appearance of the horse in the morning and make the men famous.

Since its initial cutting, the horse and the Frog Firle Farm acres were acquired by the National Trust in 1991 and the carving has been scoured several times. The first renovation was after it had been camouflaged during the war in 1940 to confuse enemy airmen.

East Sussex County Council scoured the horse in the 1980s - during which they changed the position of the legs from standing to prancing to help prevent movement of the chalk rubble used to fill the figure.

The latest scouring for this 90ft hill figure was in 1993.

MATE FOR THE LONG MAN

There is a legend that on the same escarpment as the White Horse stands Eve, a companion to the Long Man of Wilmington. There is no evidence of this though from a distance, but some say that on the landscape a woman can be viewed lying on her back with the white horse on her right leg and a small woodland in an appropriate V shape in between the two legs.

Another possibility is the V-shape hill is the same as that on which the Long Man of Wilmington is found, indicating the position of another chalk-carved figure on the V.

LEGENDS AT ST ANDREW'S

The account of the placement of Alfriston Church, reputedly set during the 14th century, is a curious story. It tells of when the first stones were being laid in a field west of the main street called Savyne Croft. The stones were magically transported each night to the east, to a field called the Tye, where they are now.

The builders couldn't decide whether this was the work of God or the Devil until four pure white oxen were spotted on the Tye by a wise man, lying rump to rump in the shape of a cross.

This decided the matter and the cruciform shape of the church that is now called the Cathedral of the Downs. However, others also claim that particular title and churches, such as Durham Cathedral, have a similar legend concerning their building.

SAINT LEWINNA

Although the church is dedicated to St Andrew, it also has associations with St Lewinna, a virgin martyr killed by a heathen Saxon about 690 AD and buried there until her remains were stolen by a monk called Balger from the Priory of Bergue St Winox and taken to Flanders in 1058.

Balgarus landed at Cuckmere Haven at Easter time and with his scribe, Drogo, made his way on recommendation to a church assumed today to be Alfriston, for Easter Mass, and stole the bones of St Lewinna, leaving only a few finger bones. It isn't certain that Alfriston was the church Balger visited though it is the most probable.

When he landed he was told he was at Sevordt, probably now Seaford, before he went three leagues (about a mile and a half in those days) inland to find the church in the story which he was told was dedicated to St Andrew. Other churches dedicated to St Andrew that have been claimed to be the visiting point of Balgarus are Jevington, Beddingham, Lewes and Bishopstone.

If the location of the church in the story is in fact Alfriston, this has bearing upon the existence of a building there before the date of the current building. Drogo also records that St Lewinna was martyred and buried in the same place indicating an even earlier date of a church in the region, despite a lot of hostility towards Christians in the county at the time of her martyrdom. Sussex was the last of the Saxon counties to be converted to christianity.

WE WON'T BE DRUV

The actual location of these engaging Sussex scenes is uncertain, but they may be seen as typical of their time.

A village parliament is seen above, whilst colourfully clothed labourers focus on their immediate needs.

THERE'S A SHIP ASHORE!

Twice in the year 1747 this cry roused local people to their favourite pastime - witnessing maritime disasters and plundering the remains. On May 21st, on the cliffs above Cuckmere Haven, men of Alfriston were among those who saw the *St Paul*, Commander R. Ragg, en route from London to America with a cargo reputedly worth £20,000 crossing Seaford Bay. They helped recapture her after she was boarded by men of a French privateer that had been lurking nearby on the lookout for a fresh victim.

A dispute over the distribution of prize money led to a notable court case and thus the names of James Batchelor, Stephen Peirce (cooper) and Samuel Virgoe (cordswainer) of Alfriston have come down to us in the list of claimants.

Only six months later another great vessel *La Nuestra de Los Remedios* (aka *La Nympha Americana*) passing the Sussex coast was wrecked on the beach not far from Cuckmere Haven. As one nautical journalist recorded . . . being very richly laden it drew some thousands of people to the place for the sake of plunder, the weather being excessively cold and wet . . . there is hardly a village for several miles around the place that would not have had one or two died or broke their limbs at the wreck.

CHARLESTON MANOR

For a number of years this lovely old house in its secluded setting at the edge of Friston Forest was the home of the celebrated portrait painter Sir Oswald Birley (1880-1952).

Sir Oswald's sitters included King George V and Queen Mary, King George VI and Queen Elizabeth, our present Queen and the Duke of Edinburgh, Sir Winston Churchill (and other Prime Ministers), Lord Louis Mountbatten along with General Eisenhower and Field Marshal Montgomerey.

Sir Oswald's wife, the former Miss Rhoda Lecky Pike of County Carlow, Eire, was a patron of the arts that included ballet, music and theatre and for several years in the 1960s was the inspiration for some very successful festivals. Whether within the great double barn where art was displayed and read, or meeting distinguished gardeners in the beautiful grounds beyond, for a while each year Charleston bloomed again.

6. *Society and smuggling*

SMUGGLING WAYS

If you wake at midnight, and hear
a horse's feet,
Don't go drawing back the blind,
or looking in the street.
Them that ask no questions isn't
told a lie.
Watch the wall, my darling, while
the Gentlemen go by!
   Five and twenty ponies,
   Trotting through the dark -
   Brandy for the Parson,
   'Baccy for the Clerk;
   Laces for a lady, letters for a spy,
Watch the wall, my darling, while
the Gentlemen go by!

Opening verses from
A SMUGGLER'S SONG
by Rudyard Kipling.

A prominent feature of the local economy from the 1600s, in the lower Cuckmere regions, was the illicit trade of incoming and outgoing cargoes.

Amid the frugal period after the Napoleonic Wars of the early 1800s many of the local populace reverted to smuggling to stimulate their life-styles. The maze of country tracks and downland hideouts played havoc with Customs Officers attempting to regulate the dark cargos. Whole communities would be involved, artisans, clergy and landowners. It was only with the trial of alleged ring-leader Stanton Collins in 1831, plus the presence of troops, that smuggling was finally eradicated.

SMUGGLING AND STANTON COLLINS

Mention Alfriston and its association with smuggling inevitably arises and one man memorably sticks out from that dire period in the parish. Stanton Collins had arrived in Alfriston in 1823 with his parents from Hailsham, where they had been successful in business as butchers. A tall, bulky man with unkempt, almost black hair and high cheek bones, their only son was an educated man, but with drive and zest that circumstances developed into a sorry trend of his character.

When troops left the area after 1815 a lawless period of hardship ensued locally. Social rebellion, barn raids and arson, and the legendary smuggling trade associated with his name, Collins was finally arrested riding through Lewes one evening. Anticipating his fate he had prepared his domestic effects should he be apprehended. He was tried at the Winter Assizes in Lewes mid December 1831 and convicted of stealing sacks of barley - ironically from his brother-in-law - at Litlington. Lord Alderson sentenced Collins to seven years transportation. Aged 35 years Collins was sent to Tasmania aboard the *Lord William Bentinck*.

He returned to Sussex in 1837, but not to Alfriston. There is no subsequent account of Stanton's wife Keturah or their pair of healthy children, also named Stanton (born 1826) and Keturah (born 1824). The youngsters had been baptised at St Andrew's by Rev Bernard John Ward, the young vicar of Berwick, on Monday September 18th 1826.

Accounts of his later life vary, but Edna and Mac McCarthy seem to have the most thorough material, although duplication of names conflict. An 1841 census shows a Stanton Collins employed as man-servant by the Rector of Herstmonceux; in 1851 he became a footman. He died in 1878 aged 82 years.

Sta(u)nton Collins was baptised at Guestling in 1792, but may have been born at Fairlight.

The name Stanton runs in the family, he was the son of Elizabeth and John who lived mainly at Herstmonceux and Wartling. Their parents were Edward Collins and Ann Stanton, who wed in 1753 in Kent.

Stanton, infamous smuggler, had two cousins also named Stanton. One born at Chiddingly in 1796 and a Stanton born a few years earlier at Etchingham. This intriguing headstone at All Saints, Herstmonceux, was thought to be that of Stanton and a second family. Inclusion of the son Robert foils the record. There is a headstone at St Mary Magdalene, Wartling, to James Stanton Collins.

Members of the so-called Alfriston Gang have been named as
Robert Adams, Lewis Aucock, Stanton Collins, Jack Figg,
George Huggett, James Huggett, John Huggett, William Pearson,
John Reeds, Samuel Thorncraft and William Trigwell.

MILTON FIRE.

Near Alfriston.

£200. REWARD.

WHEREAS
On SUNDAY EVENING last,
THE

BARNS

AND RICKS,
At Milton Farm, in the Parish of Arlington,
Were maliciously SET on FIRE.

Whoever will give Information against the Offender or Offenders, so that he or they may be brought to Justice, shall receive TWO HUNDRED POUNDS REWARD, over and above all other Rewards; to be paid on Conviction.

F. H. GELL.

ES, 12th December, 1831.

BAXTER, PRINTER, LEWES.

SOCIAL UNREST

This poster from 1834 exemplifies the period of poverty fuelled by the mechanisation of traditional agricultural methods of labour.

A decade of hardship and reactions by fraught landowners and poor farming folk sparked an all-time low for the local community at large.

Milton Barn was rebuilt in 1874 and is seen now - splendid in its robust flintwork.

In April 2006 Milton Barn and the adjoining Plovers Barn were put on the market with Winkworths locally and around their 54 central London offices.

The sumptuous 12-acre site was offered at £1.8m.

Subscribers to the mid-1800s Union Prosecuting Society were estate and farm owners who became desperate to preserve their own businesses and life-styles.

MEETING FOR THE
REPEAL OF THE POOR LAW.
NOTICE.

A PUBLIC MEETING will be held in the School Room, Star Lane, ALFRISTON, Sussex, on Wednesday Evening, the 11th of April, 1838, at 7 o'clock, for the purpose of promoting Petitions to Parliament for the Repeal of the POOR LAW AMENDMENT ACT. A Gentleman from a distance has engaged to attend and address the meeting relative to the repeal of the above Act.

As the Poor---and as well Englishmen of all classes---are so much interested in the measure, it is hoped that the labouring classes around, and especially such as pertain to those parishes that are united to the EASTBOURNE Poor Law Union---of which ALFRISTON is one---will generally attend the meeting.

HAVING been called to preside last year at two public meetings, numerously attended, held at ALFRISTON, for the purpose of Petitioning Parliament for an alteration in the POOR LAW AMENDMENT ACT; and having lately received a Requisition signed by several persons from different Parishes around, to call a Public Meeting for the purpose of Petitioning Parliament for the Repeal of the said Poor Law Amendment Act; and believing that Act to be both unconstitutional and unscriptural, and as such, in the main, exceedingly injurious to the welfare of the British Nation; and being fully persuaded also as to any real good, the said law cannot be amended, I have, in accordance with the above requisition, appointed a public meeting, as specified in the above notice: and it is hoped that a candid hearing will be given to all that may address the meeting, whether for or against the repeal of the above Act.

As the carrying into execution a public meeting must of necessity create some expence—though in this instance but little is anticipated---in order to meet the same, it is proposed that a collection be made at the meeting---that is, in a voluntary way---and that no person give more than one penny, and it is hoped no one will give less; and should not this prove sufficient to cover expences, the deficiency shall be provided by me; and should any surplus arise, it shall be presented to some public charity.

CHARLES BROOKER.

ALFRISTON, SUSSEX.

BREADS, PRINTER, HAILSHAM.

POOR LAW REFORM

The mid-1800s was a difficult time for the village. The troops had left with their trade and local industry was in decline. The Industrial Revolution compounded the confines of the rural community at large.

7. *In uniform*

Local men enlisting at Queen's Square Brighton.
Perhaps pondering what lay ahead for them . . .

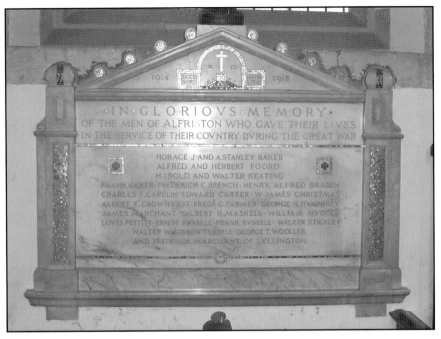

The names of local men who served, and in certain cases paid the ultimate
sacrifice, during two world wars is recorded in St Andrew's Church.

Alfriston Roll of Honour

1939 — On Active Service — 1945

Frank Allen	Leonard Carter	Geoffry Hilton	John Hugh O'Neil	Charles Henry Taylor
John Barnard	George Christmas	Fred Hughes	Harold Pierce	Geoffry Willm Tingley
Geoffry Blake Barnard	Charles Cole	Leslie Hughes	Gerald Percy Pierce	David Trehearne
Peter Dennis Barnard	Gerald Cole	Jock Hugill	Victor Peach	Ruth Trehearne
+CHARLES BATTEN+	Joseph Cole	Philippa Hugill	Arthur Kingsley Permain	Frank Tuppen
Jack Battle	James Dobson	Arthur Humphrey	David Kenneth Pettit	Walter Turrell
Brian Beales	+JOSEPH DOBSON+	Frederick Humphrey	John Pettit	William Turrell
Percy Charles Berry	Mary Dobson	Sylvia Jane Johnson	Edgar Reed	+ALBERT VINES+
Eric George Brook	Joseph Dumbrell	George Hamilton Knott	Fred Reed	Fred Wakeham
Albert Brownell	Willm George Edwards	Cha's Edward Levett	Jack Reed	Richard Wakeham
Arthur Brownell	Peter Fitchett	Ronald Albert Levett	Roland Reed	Frank Walder
William Cha's Brownell	+SYDNEY FULLER+	John Coats Lower	Ronald James Reed	Robert Walder
Joan Buckland	Cha's Edward Funnell	Sydney Lower	John Robarts	Stanley Walder
Fred Burgess	John Gillebrand	Harry Marchant	John Rush	Michael Walton
Herbert Burgess	Reginald James Harmer	ANTHONY MERRITT+	Alfred Sandles	Robert Walton
Kenneth George Burgess	Richard Harriot	Frank Norman	Sidney Selvey	Frank Wassell
Peter Burgess	Richard Hilton	Frederick Page	William Smith	George Weekes
Arthur Burton	Ronald Hilton	+RONALD PAGE+	Arthur James Sop	William Weekes
James Lewis Butland	Frederick Hilton	Theodore Page	Reginald Sop	
William Butland	Jack Hilton	Gabrielle O'Neil	Victor Stone	
Arthur Burgess				

Script E.M. Jackson
MARCH 1951

In Memory of
Flight Lieutenant CHARLES BATTEN DFC
101055, Royal Air Force Volunteer Reserve
who died age 25
on 24 September 1945
Son of Elijah and Jessie Eugenia Batten,
of Alfriston.
Remembered with honour
ALFRISTON (ST. ANDREW) CHURCHYARD

In Memory of
Trooper JOSEPH DOBSON
7951087, 142nd (7th Bn. The Suffolk Regt.) Regt.,
Royal Armoured Corps
who died age 19
on 21 February 1943.
Remembered with honour
MEDJEZ-EL-BAB WAR CEMETERY

In Memory of
Gunner SIDNEY RICHARD PETER FULLER
14525524, 1 Field Regt., Royal Artillery
who died age 20
on 16 March 1944
Son of William Sidney and Lillian Jessie Fuller,
of Alfriston.
Remembered with honour
CASSINO WAR CEMETERY

In Memory of
Pilot Officer ANTHONY GEORGE MERRITT
108955, 33 Sqdn., Royal Air Force Volunteer Reserve
who died age 19
on 04 July 1942
Son of Bertram Thomas Barnett Merritt and Phyllis Merritt.
of Deans Place, Alfriston.
Remembered with honour
ALAMEIN MEMORIAL

In Memory of
Gunner RONALD JAMES PAGE
809019, 15 Field Regt., Royal Artillery
who died age 31
on 12 June 1944
Son of Harry and Dorcas Page,
of Alfriston.
Remembered with honour
MORO RIVER CANADIAN WAR CEMETERY

In Memory of
Gunner ALBERT JAMES VINES
910156, 22 Field Regt., Royal Artillery
who died age 35
on 16 September 1944
Son of Albert and Eleanor Vines; husband of Evelyn Vines,
of Alfriston.
Remembered with honour
GRADARA WAR CEMETERY

COCKLESHELL HERO

The headstones at St Andrew's mark the passing of many notable personalities, each with their own families and roles in public life.

Heroic Royal Marine William Sparks DSO, a modest man, was part of the ten-man team that on December 11th 1942 paddled in kayaks 10 miles along the river Gironde in the Bay of Biscay to attack enemy vessels with limpet mines at Bordeaux. They travelled over five nights to avoid detection.

Eight of the Marines were either drowned or executed. The attack eventually sunk or disabled five merchant ships, but only Bill Sparks and his CO survived. The famous operation was immortalised in the 1955 film *Cockleshell Heroes*.

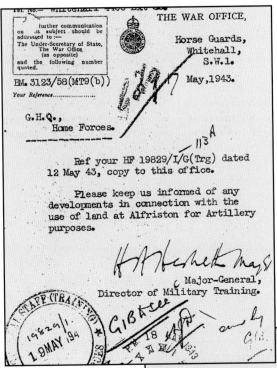

The Canadian Army established an artillery range at Alfriston, The firing points were on Westover Hill to the east of the village and the fall of shot on the other side of the village to the west.

As far as is known there was only one shell that fell short - this killed a pig in Harmer's Farm.

An Auxiliary Fire Service Station was set up in what had been the Youth Club at the bottom of the White Lodge grounds.

This became a bungalow owned by Miss Turner.

WARTIME RECOLLECTIONS

Shortly after the outbreak of WWII some 120 children from the Shadwell district in London were allocated to Alfriston homes, bringing a fresh dialect to the rural environs.

There are numerous memories still of how they acclimatised to baths, meals and schools and also of sleeping conditions as apparently some of the Londoners were used to sleeping under their parents' beds. However, in 1940 the evacuees were moved to South Wales once the dangers of invasion became more apparent.

Alfriston was devoid of sandbags and the ARP siren in Seaford was audible enough for the village. A Home Guard unit was formed and those not on active service took up defence roles and training.

Both enemy and Allied aeroplanes were involved in action over the village and some crashed heavily. A Spitfire came down near Lullington Cottages and its pilot died on the way to hospital. A Wellington bomber was lost with all its crew at Clapham Farm. One night a Heinkel 111 pilot perished after his parachute failed to open over Cradle Hill. An Me109 dived into Berwick brickyard and a Dornier Do215 attacked the dormant aerodrome at Milton Street.

Early in 1945 all 27 Allied airmen aboard lost their lives in a pair of tragic incidents involving two Dakota C-47 transport aircraft striking the Downs near the Long Man.

MAYOR ELECTED

The presence of troops in the district once again brought an added dimension to the village.

A novel event to elect a mock mayor was held at the Star Inn in September 1943. Licensee Mr W. Pease had overseen the sale of votes at 3d each. Monies totalled were to pay for gift parcels to each of 180 Allied Prisoners of War. The final sale of votes had been concluded by 10.00pm that Saturday night.

The failed candidate was Sergeant Wally RA with 1,984 votes - he declared to be relieved of the role as he was leaving the area shortly.

Mr Pease, the new mayor, with 1990 votes, was robed with all old-time ceremony by Lt Colonel Jones OBE, RA, the Officer Commanding.

An auction of fruit and farm produce added to the banter between villagers and army. The mayor closed by saying he would not take up office as he was going to Blackpool soon. The buffoonery, however, raised the sum of £90.00 for our Prisoners of War.

Saturday February 5th 1944. 13.20 hours. A ploughed field at The Rails, Alfriston, was the scene of Boeing Fortress 231244 being seriously damaged. The mighty B-17 bomber was returning from an operational flight when it force-landed with engine trouble. All ten crew survived the crash.

WARTIME RELICS

The village could have been blown apart had this naval mine exploded after being washed four miles inland in October 1942. River authority employee Roger Walker and a colleague strung ropes across the river to harness the offending mine that now acts as a collection facility beside the Tye.

Scores of WWII concrete dragons teeth anti-tank bollards were collected up and moved to the recreation ground to keep vehicles off the plot. Defence blocks were located at Wingrove Corner, where some obstacles remain amidst the undergrowth.

HMS ALFRISTON

One of the Ton-class minesweepers HMS Alfriston, order code MP2701 (M1103) originated on April 29th 1953. The vessel was eventually scrapped in 1988 after being transferred to the Royal New Zealand Navy.

ARMY CAMPS

Colourful scenes like this WWI encampment on the Downs have been all too often an aspect of the district and provided commercial values to local traders and employees. With the nearby embarkation ports and ample training terrain troops fraternised and integrated with the local community. Numerous former Armed Services personnel returned to civilian life near the coast.

RIVER ACTIVITY

The iron anchor and headstone of 'Capt.' William Nye lies at St Andrew's Church. He was reputedly one of the last boatmen to carry cargo along the river.

Recorded in the view below, during Cuckmere bridging exercises at Frog Firle in 1913, are members of the Household Cavalry.

8. *Around and about*

Traditional values - quality of life . . .

ARTISTS' HAVEN

The village environs have for generations attracted painters and photographers to record the lovely scenes found on the downland. Albert Robert Quinton (1883-1934) produced more than two thousand famous paintings (some seen opposite) of seaside resorts, spas, pretty towns and villages around the country, to be printed as postcards by Salmon of Sevenoaks, Tuck & Sons, and others.

In 1895 he cycled from Lands End to John O'Groats in search of material; he was said to use popular views time and again over the years by up-dating with new dress styles and other social changes.

INTRIGUE ON FOOT

Echoes of the past can be imagined from the array of associations gleaned from name plates and dating.

In the days before the public fire service insurance companies provided emergency vehicles to attend their clients' properties first.

INTRIGUE EN MASSE

Numerous name plates reveal trades and activities from the 1880s when the village was more of a commercial centre for the district.

INTRIGUE AT LARGE

The Alfriston neighbourhood is ready-made to investigate - exploration may be on foot or delving into old record documents.

OFF THE BEATEN TRACK

Among the charms of Alfriston are the unexpected twittens and short cuts that one comes across. Here are some glimpses through open doors of passages linking the High Street and the Tye.

Of equal interest are the array of site and property names reflecting the village's past life-styles.

HIGH AND OVER

Correctly named High and Over, not Hindover, the downland highway from Alfriston to Seaford has become part of the commuter network these days. Motorists are able to experience the Cuckmere Valley panorama and ambience in all its moods.

Traditionally the thoroughfare had been an ordeal for farm wagons and travellers, it was often impossible to use the steep chalk-rutted by-way during spring and winter periods.

Ascent of the slopes was serious enough to be competitive for motorcyclists seen in this May 1921 Speed Trials event.

Updating recreation into the 21st century it is hang gliders who often frequent the escarpment brooding over the Cuckmere.

CORONATION TREES

Almost synonymous with the Market Cross in the village is the central chestnut tree that is said to have been planted to commemorate the coronation of Queen Victoria in 1837.

That being so the dominating leafy spread has been the venue for decades of photographs, postcards, courting, reunions, festivals, and social events since the 1860's advent of popular photography.

Less well known are the origins of the chestnut tree by the wooden finger post at Peachey's Corner.

The ill-cared for tree was in fact planted to record the coronation of Queen Elizabeth II in 1952.

VILLAGE HALLS

On January 28th 1988 the new community hall was officially opened by the Right Hon. Lord Healey CH MBE. The refurbishment and extension around Alfriston War Memorial Hall was carried out by W. Llewellyn & Sons Ltd. National funds had been made available towards the project.

This former School Room and adjoining house, to the right, dates from 1844 - a classroom had been joined at the back in 1817. There used to be an old WWI army social hut here, paid for by gratuities by former soldiers to hold socials, etc.

The United Reformed Church Hall has been known as the Congregational Church Hall and the Chapel Memorial Hall. Prior to that it was known as the Gun Room.

In the early 1800s troops stored a large gun there that was periodically taken up to Kings Ride and Winton Chalk Pit for practice.

THE SANCTUARY

In mid-1912 a detached house was being built near Comp Barn at Winton Street, almost a half-mile inland north from Alfriston.

During trenching works for the home and western boundary of the acre plot workmen discovered scores of Anglo-Saxon skeletons, with fine bronze fibrillae amongst other artefacts like gilt beads and glassware.

In all 120 graves were excavated; the find is recorded in Sussex Archaeological Society Collections Vol I vi. The roadside wooden crucifix was placed there in April 1919 by Miss Alice S. Gregory for whom the house named *The Sanctuary* was built.

During WWII there were three eight-inch Howitzers located around Winton Street to protect the district.

In 1946 housing developers sought to capitalise on a military metalled highway laid out across chalky Roman Road seen here. The Army road went west onto the top of the Downs.

This plan was halted by H.S. Martin, ESCC Chief Clerk, who described the tank road as one of the worst eye-sores in the area.

ALL ROADS TO ALFRISTON

Alfriston has always been a popular venue for outings, indeed today it is the parish economy. Members of Mid-Sussex Fire Brigade are depicted off duty. The terraced homes behind were occupied as Wellington barracks in the 1800s.

Nowadays with old photographs it is background that can be of prime interest.

Seaford Band are seen playing at an evening concert in August 1949 - and the Johnny Spice Big Band perform on August Bank Holiday 2005.

THAT ALFRISTON LION

During 2002 the ship's figurehead was removed for expert restoration by Rev Frank Fox-Wilson, whose interests include wood carving. The lion had 19 coats of paint and extensive wood damage. The rejuvenation is archived in a booklet the Restoration of the Lion Figurehead 2002-2004. Reportedly the symbolic carving was brought from a Cuckmere Haven 1690s wreck by smugglers.

Finally, on February 7th 2004, the elegant restored woodwork was re-positioned at the less vulnerable northerly side of the Star Inn. Lord Healey performed the unveiling ceremony before an assembled crowd.

1845 Schoolmaster's house

SCHOOLING

The original school in Alfriston was started as a Church School in 1817 by Rev J. Capper, Vicar of Wilmington, in co-operation with Rev Thomas Williams, Vicar of Alfriston 1784-1821. Classes were first held in the chancel of St Andrew's; pupils came from neighbouring villages that in 1818 had a combined population of 1,800 people including 300 children.

In 1820 schooling moved into a property built by Rev Capper, on the site of the new War Memorial Hall. Classrooms have been sited on the Tye, behind Star Assembly Rooms, at the Lower's Garage site and finally the North Road school that opened in September 7th 1904 with 143 pupils from the neighbourhood.

A new school hall and facilities were finished in early 2006.

HIGHWAY HAZARDS

The picturesque raised footpath north out of the village was created by Dutch engineers in the mid-1920s to elevate pedestrians above the seasonal floods that blight the area.

Into the 21st century, when vehicle widths and through traffic had increased considerably, the C39 had become increasingly hazardous. Norman Baker MP sought action on widening the road and a local landowner donated part of a field by the old brickworks to encourage the scheme.

However, in January 2006 the ESCC responded that this problem acted as a traffic calming measure, forcing vehicles into the middle of the road. They would only concede to introduce clearer 'narrow road' signs as the flint wall perceived additional narrowing.

ALFRISTON'S MOCK MILL

An intriguing article in a late 2004 edition of Alfriston's *Cuckmere News* began to unravel the mystery of the North Street car park tower (right).

Talking with Dick Wakeham (died 2006) one of the parish's longest-standing residents the editor mentioned the folly that has variously been noted as an armoury, an ice-house, memorial, a shot tower, store, a dovecote or a lock-up prison.

From the 1700s the Dene, and now Little Dene, were one house, with a rear garden out across the now short stay car park. In the late Victorian era the Dene was owned by a Mr Elliott and he is said to have built the tower (styled on the 1835 tower mill near Deans Place?) as a play-house for his three daughters. The folly had two floors with cross beams, topped with a round stone to raise the roof.

As the years passed along (Pike's Directory 1940 has a Miss E.M. Elliott resident at the Dene) the large garden became overgrown with bramble and ivy and the tower could not be seen.

Mr Wakeham said that when the site was being cleared it was decided to burn off the ivy and the tower re-emerged; alas, though, the floors were burnt out.

Over the ensuing years the edifice has been the topic of numerous theories. The site has now been researched via ESRO TDE/14 as built on the site of the late 1700s post mill there. Use of the low-lying mill was eclipsed by Mill Bank tower mill built in 1835 near Deans Place - seen opposite c1980 as a private home.

Between 1823-1846+ the 0.9 acre Dene plot (the car park) was owned by miller William Woodhams. Nearby a wall engraving reading WMW 1822 is attributed to Mr Woodhams.

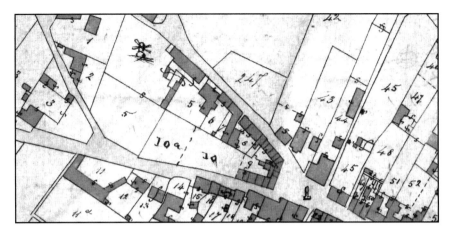

OF MILLS AND MILLERS

From the 1800s a post mill was sited from behind the Dene in North Street. The Market Cross along with William Woodhams post mill are seen on this 1843 tithe map, reproduced with the permission of the County Archivist ESRO, copyright reserved.

There was also a mill on Windover Hill by the Long Man. From the 1700s-1870s the vulnerable Downs site saw a sequence of ten mills destroyed by storm or fire.

It is said the fate of a 1830s mill there had been sealed when the miller refused to co-operate with smugglers and the mill became a victim of a curious incendiary attack. In the 1840s the miller was Thomas Boys of Milton Street.

The final mill on Windover Hill was destroyed during a storm in November 1879, its relics being shown on maps to the 1930s. Mill foundations and barn site at OS.537035 can be found just past Windover Reservoir.

An artists impression of Windo'or Mill.

WINDMILLS OF THEIR TIME

Alfriston tower mill, at Frog Firle, was erected 1834 and was operated by Daniel Sudbury who lived at the Post Office. The tower is seen below around 1905 when she ceased grinding corn. The site was originally named Rabbit Bank, but more recently known as Mill Bank, Meal Bank or Mere bank.

In 1910 the shell of the mill was refurbished as a feature of a private home. Mill House was occupied in the 1960s by Dr Yeo and his family.

Rabbit Bank mill seen from Deans Place, White Way.

PLONK BARN

The sturdy flint barn, dated 1608, was resurrected as a private abode in 1986 and re-named Great Meadow Barn. It backs onto the sunken cattle track that leads to Lullington Church. De Warde's map of 1618 shows Plonke Bridge and on a hill east of the river is The Plonke House on land owned by the Earl of Dorset. Derivatives = *Plonk* as alcoholic wine maybe made therein, *planke* a property possibly being weather-boarded originally.

The imposing tree-arched highway from Plonk Barn to Peachey's Corner is known locally as The Beach (indicating the former expanse of the tidal river) - the trees colloquially as The Cathedral.

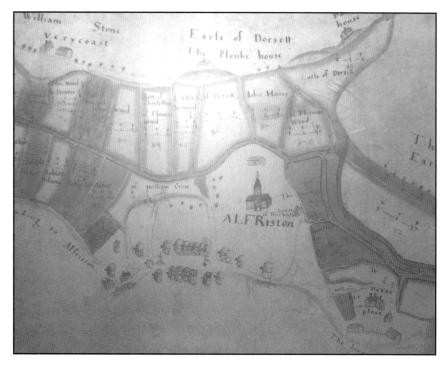

DE WARDE'S MAP OF 1618

Cartography is an intriguing art, particularly in the case of the Cuckmere Valley with its Roman and Saxon heritage. This fascinating representation is one of the earliest accessible with copious features from Long Bridge to Deans Place. The map, now at Chatsworth House, was photographed by Rev Walter Budgen in the early 1900s. ESRO AMS 5764/11. It is also known as Budgen's map.

Plonk Lane is nowadays overgrown with thicket and is impassable. Yet one of Alfriston's oldest residents Mrs Evelyn Vines, born 1914 and having only lived in Alfriston, recalls playing in the lane as a youngster. Dirk Bogarde in his early 1930's memoirs describes the gully as strewn with shrubbery, as one of their childhood haunts and speaks of its smuggling folklore. Local man Barry Norman recalls cattle using Plonk Barn in the 1960s, with the lane being clear of shrubbery. Barry's grandmother came from Wiltshire to settle in Alfriston. He bemoans that people, like himself, born in the village can no longer afford homes to live there.

Prominent above is The Plonke House, but the property had probably been long demolished by 1845. Similarly various farm barns there had become derelict, burnt or blown down. (ESRO Lullington tenement Analysis). Plonk Barn on Yeakell & Gardner's 1780 map is shown south of the lane's lower access and rights of way continue to be an issue there. The upper access is broad beside Lullington Church and cottages onto the Wilmington Road - The Street. This map spells Tullington for Lullington and Littleington for Litlington.

AN ENHANCED ENGRAVING FROM 1830 SHOWING THE MAZE
OF TRACKS THAT SERVED THE COMMUNITY -
WITH TURNPIKES AND RAILWAY ADDED.

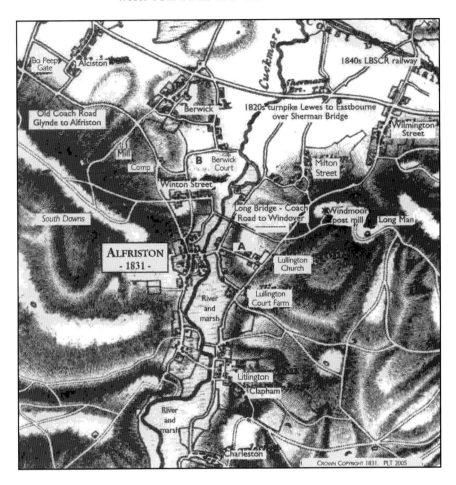

A is the overgrown sunken farm track from Plonk Barn to Lullington Church.
The thoroughfare is shown here prominent to its then usage.

B indicates how the highway from Berwick Court turned west towards Comp
Barn before bearing south to appear midway at Winton Street, onto Alfriston.

ALFRISTON, NEW ZEALAND

Extracts from the commemorative book The Vintage Years. By Lorna W. Wilson. A Record of Alfriston-Brookby since the 1850s. Kindly provided by Natalie Mackenzie, Library Administrator at Alfriston School, Auckland.

The Papakura Valley, the name by which Alfriston and Brookby was first known after European settlement comprises of four groups - peat swamp, the flats, fertile hillsides and the poorer ridges. The now Alfriston area takes in quite a large piece of what was known as the Takanini Swamp.

The prospect of plenty of work, better living conditions and room to develop encouraged people to embark on the great adventure of over five months sailing to New Zealand.

1875 saw the arrival in the Papakura Valley of Dr George and Mrs Eliza Bodle who had left their home in Alfriston, Sussex, together with their three children. Mrs Bodle's widowed mother Mrs Darroch accompanied the family there with their maid eventually occupying the front rooms in the home built in Alfriston. In 1876 the Duchess of Argyll (667 tons) and the Jane Gifford (558 tons) were the first pioneer ships to arrive in the Waitemata Harbour, Auckland. Ten days later the vessel St George arrived off shore.

Dr George Bodle.

Mrs Bodle, the daughter of a Major in the British Army, was born in Lucknow. Dr Bodle who fulfilled the duties of a ships doctor on the voyage to New Zealand did not seek to create a practice there, but gave a long and faithful service to the residents and gum diggers in his capacity as a 'free' doctor.

How grateful many of the settlers must have been having his skilled ministrations during the births of their children, as well as the fevers so many endured in those early years.

As well as building his own lovely home, which unfortunately has not withstood the passage of time, Dr Bodle and other residents built the Meeting House as it became known - originally as a Church of Christ establishment. Bushy Park, as the farm is still named, was an extensive area stretching from the Anglican Church to the junction of Ranfurly and Stratford Roads, bordering the Alfriston Road opposite the church, including the school, store and now Stone property. The community also had good reason to be grateful to the Bodle's as land for a school was willingly provided. The later owners of Bushey Park Mr and Mrs Alex Green farm 110 acres and preserved ten of their acreage in its natural bush state as the original occupiers would have known the plot.

Dr and Mrs Bodle would have been delighted to know that school children over the decades, and more recently Guides and Scouts, have spent many happy hours amongst the Puriri's, Kauri's, Rimu's and other native trees.

ALFRISTON, AUCKLAND

This gravestone at the Anglican church carries the name Bodle. The inscription reads -

In Loving Memory of
George Edward Bodle. L.R.G.P.
Late of Bushy Lodge Alfriston.
Passed away 22nd May 1916.
Aged 72.
Also his loved Wife
Eliza Jeannette Bodle.
Born 1845. Died 1923.

The small timber property opposite is all that remains of George Bodle's original meeting house.

The Community School house is the first school built around 1893. They celebrated a centenary in 1994. In late February 2006 the former school at Alfriston was moved to a new plot. The assembled school was able to watch behind the safety barriers as the huge truck it was placed on began a brief passage across the asphalt playground and was parked on the new site. They left it on stilts while the contractors prepared pilings for it to settle on.

Local people said it was sad to think that a building that occupied the same ground for over 100 years was moved from its privileged place by the cross-roads. It will retain its old character and be part of the new performing arts centre.

The village that Bodle and others planned did not eventuate. The crossroads upon which the community house stands was once thought to be in a good position for a village. It remains essentially rural, but life-style blocks of Papakura and Manurewa creep ever nearer.

The Anglican Church was dedicated in 1877.

A LAST DELVE INTO THE DISTRICT

The Seaford bus. At the Market Cross people sometimes caught the Seaford bus that called only twice a day and carried parcels as well as passengers.

The building in West Street known as the Old Forge was at one time utilised as a bus garage.

THEN AND NOW IN HIGH STREET

Here are two views of the same part of the High Street taken some 75 years apart.

Unstead & Sons Carriers sign can be seen to the left of the earlier view. The cottages were created from the former Steamer Inn, in old Wealden style without an upper floor.

These venerable buildings demonstrate the timelessness of the village and the dedication of those who strive - and have striven to - keep its historic aspect.

A final look at Alfriston.
Ron Levett may have walked on water to photo his wife Betty
during the October 2000 floods at North Street.

Scenes by Ron Levett that would win awards in a photo society competition - showing the extent of typical floods that add to the beauty and perils of the Alfriston environs.
North Street car park above and looking north off Plonk Bridge below.

6oo Years of history...

Charter 6oo

...A Whole Weekend of Celebrations
9-11 June 2006

The community spent months organising the Charter 600 celebrations. Highly successful events took place over three days also on the Tye and around the village.

9. *Nearby villages*

Traditional downland routes are perpetuated by the
splendid Cuckmere Community Bus services.
In mid-2006 the 40 volunteer drivers from Britain's
oldest community bus service were awarded the
Queen's Award commendation for 30 years endeavour.

DOWNLAND SPECTACLES

Oxen were used in the Cuckmere pastures until the 1940s. It is said they were less troublesome than horses and could be eaten when they were past their prime for farming uses.

In 1972 the Royal Oak public house at Milton Street was re-named The Sussex Ox after the downland trojans.

Wilmington's mysterious lanky 230ft tall Long Man oversees activities as time goes by . . .

TOURISM WITHOUT TRAFFIC

Many amongst us were all too familiar with the old coach road (Glyndebridge turnpike) under the Downs invariably being a quagmire of mud and chalk. Thus people may have been bemused initially by ESCC proposals to lay a hard surface on the ancient West Firle-Berwick section of the spring line villages Lewes to Eastbourne thoroughfare that had wearily served centuries of travellers and farm traffic.

Together with the Sussex Downs Conservation Board the county council has been trying to encourage visitors to explore the downland district by walking, horse-riding and cycling. After clearance and levelling works were completed the contractors laid limestone fines, limestone chippings, over a layer of binding material with a porous membrane that helped drainage, and the surface was then re-laid during 2004.

To add to the pleasures of the tranquil track local farmer Ian Williams began to offer groups of eight people the option of being taken along the route in a farm wagon, drawn by his pair of shire horses Ben and Harvey. The carriage can link up with the Cuckmere Community Bus service.

Tourism without Traffic chairman Michael Ann OBE took caution of the potential perils caused by off-road vehicle drivers and motor-cyclists using the bridlepath. As a rambler having sampled the new metalled surface of the former stagecoach highway one has to comment that it is almost with an uncanny ease that people can experience the park-like conditions.

Part of the charisma of walking the route is scenery like the remote Edwardian property named Beanstalk alongside the track near Firle Tower.

Beanstalk, Heighton Street.

ALCISTON

Pronounced Arlston this quaint community originated as the tun, or farmstead, of a South Saxon named Aelfsige. In the 1086 Domesday Book it is recorded as Alsistone and by 1327 as Alcistona. The manor house and lands of Alciston belonged to Battle Abbey and it was occupied by monks in transit. Court Farm House and other notable relics include the listed medieval dovecote.

The undedicated 12th century church stands on a hillock. The chancel was shortened in the 13th century - that is noted as being a reflection on the diminishing population. Traces of more recent life styles, like the Post Office, estate and farm property, add to the intrigue of this retreat under the Downs.

The imposing Abbey tithe barn at Alciston Court is one of the nation's largest at 170ft long. Aspects include a steep-pitched tiled roof and massive timber doors.

The roar of A27 traffic can be heard sadly to break the rural calm of Alciston, but ample refreshment is available at the popular Rose Cottage public house that first obtained its licence in the early 1900s.

ARLINGTON

Mention the name of this Saxon village these days may lead to an association with the reservoir there and of walks and nature studies - also of the popular Yew Tree public house or the nearby speedway circuit. The village, however, retains its rustic isolation, devoid of intrusions and main thoroughfares.

The church of St Pancras is noted for its original exterior and considerate late Victorian internal renovation along with a list of features dating back to the 14th century. The lych gate is a millennium addition.

BEDDINGHAM

The name Beddingham derives from a water meadow (hamm) occupied by a minor Saxon tribe the Beadingas. In 880AD it is recorded as Beadingahamme.

When the turnpike was commenced in 1819 of the downland villages it was Beddingham that benefited the most. The previous narrow Ranscombe Lane route under Caburn took twice as long. Note the extant mid-1819 toll cottage below.

When the railway arrived at first villagers were reluctant to use the system. A daily stagecoach and the alternative days omnibus adequately served local needs.

Into the 21st century Beddingham means that rail crossing. Traffic levels are at 30,000 vehicles daily and the construction of a flyover is due to start in autumn 2006 to replace the time-consuming railway crossing that hinders A27 travellers.

BERWICK

The landmark church of St Michael and All Angels has many absorbing features both internally and externally. Visitors may liken to the array of Bloomsbury Set murals that nearby Charleston Farmhouse that was commissioned by Dr. G. K. A. Bell, Bishop of Chichester in 1941.

On October 17th 1944 some Victorian windows were damaged as bombs blew out ornate leaded plain glass frames. The north and south aisles still have clear plate glass as it was uncertain if further damage would follow.

BERWICK

Opposite the engaging Harveys of Lewes hostelry named Cricketers Arms (above) is the village Tye, although it is little acknowledged as such these days. The nearby Sussex Ox pub has a daunting panorama towards Firle Beacon.

The 1840s creation of the London Brighton & South Coast Railway brought a fresh lease of life to this traditional downland parish when a level crossing was created and an inevitable community spawned alongside the road to Dicker.

Before the 1950s this hamlet was self-contained with an attractive commercial aura of its own. A corn mill and a variety of local traders provided services and employment. Of all the Sussex diarist accounts perhaps the most informative is *Recollections of a Sussex Parson* by Edward Boys Ellman 1815-1906 - he was the Curate, then Vicar, of Berwick.

A building can be a many-extended thing . . . The Berwick Inn walls evoke decades of topical building styles and materials.

FIRLE

The Georgian manor Firle Place was built in specially imported Caen stone from Normandy and is the Gage family traditional home. Amongst numerous matters they introduced the green plum to Britain and gave it their name.

Correctly titled West Firle, after the original village was abandoned pre-1255, the near feudal atmosphere of the main street remains quirky and quaint just off the bustle off the A27 highway.

The estate is full of interest and resides on fertile greensand and gault fields. The house is open at stated times and numerous public functions are held during the year in the grounds.

FOLKINGTON

The charm of these downland villages is perhaps personified in Folkington past when it had a parochial school and resident rector, a dairy and postal facilities of its own accord. In 1861 the parish of 1,521 acres comprised of 154 people.

Today the no-through road to St Peter's Church is best known to walkers who park near the church and can set off on a variety of paths to enjoy the splendour of the South Downs in all their moods. Stepping into the church is almost like taking a step back in time, family pews and modest fittings add to the lure of the buildings extant under the shadow of lofty woodland. The imposing former Rectory is seen above.

GLYNDE

The rural sprawl making up the Glynde estate is a curious mixture of intrigue stemming from artisan and aristocratic activity. Statuesque Glynde Place is a superb Elizabethan manor house that is open to the public. The adjacent church designed by Sir Thomas Robinson, built 1763-1765, is the only one created in a classical style and is the finest 18th-century example in Sussex.

Here in 1778 John Ellman began breeding sheep that became the now famous black-nosed Southdown flocks. Depicted below is the short-lived overhead Telpher Line that opened in October 1885. It ferried trucks by cable across a mile of meadows from Viscount Hampden's brick clay quarries to sidings at Glynde station. The nearby River Ouse has borne a variety of commercial enterprises. The distinctive forge, above, was re-built in 1907 as a farriers and the business was resurrected in 1996 by Terry Tyhurst as a general forge.

JEVINGTON

This downland district is steeped with settlements and earthworks of the South Saxons who inhabited the area.

In the 1700-1800s smuggling was rife around the village maze of tracks and hills. Kelly's 1870 lists Mrs Ruth Griffin as schoolmistress, the school seen below was built in 1846. John Seymour was landlord of the Eight Bells and Sidney Griffin the shoemaker. Herbert Goldsmith toiled as a wheelwright with John Dumbrell a shopkeeper, Mrs Mary Walters was the blacksmith and William Clay a racehorse trainer amid several local farmers under the auspices of Rev James Dunn at the church of St Andrew.

Most of these occupations have long since vacated the village, but it can be seen as typical of its neighbourhood - reaping a living off the land.

LITLINGTON

This district is nowadays perhaps best known for its role on the lower Cuckmere Valley tourist trail. Its halcyon days being in the early 1900s when village life was confined to farming and the basic needs resourced within that area.

Records from 1858 state that the parish was of only 893 acres and comprised of 105 residents. John Terry was landlord at the Plough and Harrow and William Weber was the blacksmith. The Russell family ran the 1900s Litlington Arms public house there, but it has been turned into a private house. Their iconic Pleasure Gardens and Tea Grounds remain, although the Post Office closed in the late 1960s. The popular Plough & Harrow is shown below.

LULLINGTON

The quaint 13th century Church of the Good Shepherd at Lullington is famous as one of the smallest churches in the nation.

These are the remains of a once larger place of worship that was ransacked in Cromwellian times. The present church being the former chancel. The property was restored for services in 1806 and more fully repaired in the 1890s. Seating capacity at the 16ft square church is limited to two dozen people - as seen below. Services are held there once a month.

An 1858 directory lists just 26 people resident in the sprawl of the farming parish.

SELMESTON

This South Saxon settlement takes its title from Sigehelm - victory helm - where he built his farmstead. Recorded in 1086 as Sielmestone it became Selmeston in 1242. It was pronounced Symston in the 16th century and Simson from 1765.

The undedicated flint-faced church at Selmeston was restored in 1867. The south arcade is of three bays with oak piers in 14th-century style.

The village war memorial had suffered the ravages of time and the volume of passing traffic. Funding was obtained in 2005 and the vulnerable monument has now been restored. The old village school, below, was built in 1876.

WILMINGTON

This area is well known, but uncommercialised, for the mysterious 230ft tall giant that overlooks the village. The original title of Wilmington Street indicates that it was a prime example of a Sussex street format community. Homes and trades were created alongside the thoroughfare that went inland to Wilmington Green, that was in time bisected by the 1820s turnpike road.

A saunter past the houses reveals place names like the old bakery, Post Office or the first Black Horse Inn before this trade moved towards the main road and has now become The Giant's Rest.

WILMINGTON

Whilst the Long Man keeps secret his origins a peep into an 1861 Kelly's Directory show a population of 250 people across 1,744 acres of the parish.

William Ade was grocer and draper, there was a maltster, miller, another shopkeeper and the local baker was also the registrar of births and deaths. There was a cobbler and a veterinary surgeon, also a harness maker and a blacksmith and farrier. Other folk in business were Davis Wise - pork butcher, William Geall - carpenter and Daniel Dumbrell the wheelwright.

Just imagine the bustle of that main street in the 1860s as children played, as women chattered and poultry and cattle passed by.

Seen opposite is Mr Reuben Russell, one of the last local shepherds in the 1930s.

In July 2002 an arsonist struck the Church of St Mary and St Peter. The inferno destroyed the north transept, the famed Bee and Butterfly window and rare Victorian organ.

The rest of the 12th century church was left with extensive heat, smoke and water damage. Half the roof was gutted and a new extension left badly damaged. It was not until September 2003 that parishioners were able to return to their renovated church.

BEFORE FRISTON FOREST GREW

Some 80 years ago Mr Alan Pullen was employed by the local water company as shepherd of the flocks that roamed on the hills above West Dean. The Forestry Commission acquired the area and a scheme of afforestation began in 1927 with the planting of beech, pine and sycamore. Hitherto only the West Dean trees concealed the village buildings, here the church spire and (right) a corner of the main farmhouse now known as West Dean Manor, can be identified.

SHEPHERDS AND SHEEP

The famous breed of Southdown sheep was introduced in the late 18th century only a few miles from Alfriston when Mr John Ellman succeeded in producing an animal with more tightly curled wool hitherto. So popular did it become that a society was formed. A good shepherd lived with his flock more than his family and a few simple caravan style huts survive to illustrate their way of life - one being on display at the Seven Sisters Country Park at Exceat.

The breed flourished abroad for many years.With the passing of time, however, they had become almost extinct and they are now being re-introduced at the Seven Sisters Sheep Centre at East Dean.

Index